Exercises in Translation

Exercises in Translation

Swiss–British Cultural Interchange

Joy Charnley & Malcolm Pender (eds)

18.01.07

PETER LANG

Oxford · Bern · Berlin · Bruxelles · Frankfurt am Main · New York · Wien

Bibliographic information published by Die Deutsche Bibliothek
Die Deutsche Bibliothek lists this publication in the Deutsche
Nationalbibliografie; detailed bibliographic data is available on
the Internet at ‹http://dnb.ddb.de›.

British Library and Library of Congress Cataloguing-in-Publication Data:
A catalogue record for this book is available from *The British Library*,
Great Britain, and from *The Library of Congress*, USA

Cover design: Adrian Baggett, Peter Lang AG

ISBN 3-03910-933-2
US-ISBN 0-8204-8328-1

© Peter Lang AG, International Academic Publishers, Bern 2006
Hochfeldstrasse 32, Postfach 746, CH-3000 Bern 9, Switzerland
info@peterlang.com, www.peterlang.com, www.peterlang.net

Printed in Germany

Contents

History

Literature

Foreword by the Swiss Ambassador

It is certainly not by chance that cultural interaction between the UK and Switzerland has intensified since the beginning of industrialisation and globalisation. Both have not only profoundly transformed the two countries but have, of course, also facilitated contacts.

As this series of texts indicates, both industrialisation and a broader trading environment have opened up and heightened interest in alternative realities and views. Early examples are the Swiss Alps and chalets, Robert Burns and the Scottish Highlands, although later trends go far beyond these. We might recall that Napoleon's continental blockade contributed to the emergence of the Swiss machine industry, which was modelled on British practice but eventually adopted the metric system. Yet, the adjustable spanner, a practical tool which adapts to different functions, is still called an 'Engländer' – an Englishman – in (Swiss) German. It is a direct reference to the underlying influences of the time, which started even before English became a universal language. Thus, as one reads through these texts, one is tempted to compare perceptions of early travellers with those of contemporary British and Swiss citizens who have decided to settle temporarily or permanently in their adopted 'other' country.

Mutual cultural influence – an enduring and dynamic process – might best be identified through a multidisciplinary and multi-faceted method. This was the approach chosen in the scholarship programme (2002–2004) for Swiss research fellows, scholars and creative writers which was launched, on an annual rotation basis, with five UK institutions of higher learning. The programme of five to six weeks' study and teaching assignments, sponsored by Presence Switzerland, was supported by Professor Malcolm Pender and Dr Joy Charnley of the German and French Divisions in the Department of Modern Languages at the University of Strathclyde; by Professor Rüdiger Görner of the Institute of Germanic Studies, part of the School for Advanced Studies at the University of London; by Professor Robert K. Weninger of the Department of Modern Languages at Oxford Brookes University; by Dr Peter Tame at Queen's University, Belfast and Dr Kate Griffiths at the University of Wales, Bangor.

I wish to thank all of the above, the Swiss fellows and all those who have contributed to making this programme a success. In order to reach a wider audience, Professor Malcolm Pender and Dr Joy Charnley have assembled a collection of texts which makes for fascinating reading for all those interested in British–Swiss relations.

Alexis P. Lautenberg
Ambassador of Switzerland to the UK

Joy Charnley and Malcolm Pender

Introduction

From 2002 to 2004 *Présence Suisse* funded a 'Swiss Fellow in the UK' programme in which five universities in the four regions of the United Kingdom participated: University College, Bangor, University of Wales; Queen's College, Belfast; the Institute of Germanic and Romance Studies, University of London; Oxford Brookes University; and the University of Strathclyde, Glasgow. The programme, established on the British side largely through the efforts of Professor Robert Weninger, then of Oxford Brookes and now of King's College London, enabled a Swiss writer or academic to be based in one of the five universities for four weeks and to undertake short visits to the other four over a further two weeks. Three Swiss Fellows took part in the programme: the novelist and journalist Hansjörg Schertenleib (German language) who was based in Oxford in 2002; the academic and writer Thérèse Moreau (French language) who was based in Strathclyde in 2003; and the academic and novelist Silvia Ricci Lempen (Italian and French languages) who was based in Bangor in 2004. Thus three of the official languages of Switzerland as well as academic and creative writing were represented in the programme.

It was felt that the success of the programme and the events which it generated should be marked by a volume of contributions from participants and organisers and from others involved in Swiss Studies in the United Kingdom. It also seemed appropriate to include in the celebration of this recent strengthening of the diverse cultural links between Switzerland and Britain writing by the first Scottish writer (Donal McLaughlin) and the first Swiss writer (Pedro Lenz) to participate in the Glasgow–Bern Writers' Exchange which was set up in 2004 with the stalwart participation of Dr David Kinloch (University of Strathclyde) and which enables writers to spend six months in the host city.

Switzerland and Britain, despite many differences, not least in size of population, have probably at least two traits in common: a respect for tradition allied to an innate conservatism on the one hand, and a practical approach to the management of life on the other. Arguably, a third similarity is emerging with glacier-like slowness: the federal structure of Switzerland, firmly anchored since 1848 in the modern state, is beginning to acquire, with the recent autonomies in Scotland and Wales, the semblance of a counterpart in the political arrangements of the United Kingdom. It might even be that Switzerland's plurality of languages is tentatively emerging here: the posters advertising the visits of the Fellows to Bangor were in both English and Welsh, as was required by law. Against this background, the contributions to this volume deal with aspects of perception and mediation which occur on a more personal level in the interchange between two countries. There are views of each country acquired by citizens of the other through travel or short sojourns (by Donal McLaughlin, Thérèse Moreau, Felicity Rash and Silvia Ricci Lempen); comments on the effect on their writing from writers who have adopted the other country by living there permanently (interviews with Marie-José Piguet and Silvia Ricci Lempen); and accounts of interchange through critical appreciation, translation and cultural borrowing (by Tom Hubbard, Donal McLaughlin, Malcolm Pender and Sue Wilson).

We should like to dedicate *Exercises in Translation – Swiss–British Cultural Interchange* to those whose imaginative hard work and efforts made a success of the undertaking 'Swiss Fellow in the UK'. On behalf of all who participated, we wish to express our thanks to *Présence Suisse* for funding the programme and for their financial support for this volume.

Glasgow, January 2006

Creative Writing

Thérèse Moreau

Deathwatch[1]

> This is the end, beautiful friend.
> This is the end, my only friend, the end
> Of our elaborate plans, the end
> Of everything that stands, the end
> No safety or surprise, the end
> I'll never look in your eyes again.
>
> The Doors, *The End*

Here She was in Glasgow, Scotland. She had run all that way to escape the unavoidable. She could no longer hide from disaster. Darkness would not conceal her. No doors of perception would open and protect her from the ice storm. Bubbles of happiness were exploding in the entire town. Painted people dressed in strange attires had gathered on the common lawn. Young people were chanting, raving, frantic with pleasure. The blue skies, the mildness of the air, the joyful surge of the City were to her only a lure. Here one young man in two felt that rape was a way of life and that hitting women was justifiable. Violence was lurking in the crowd, ready to find a victim. The document *Living without Fear* published a few years ago was of no use to her nor would be the discourses of the Glasgow University authorities on the 25th of November. In fact the University had decided to talk not about women but about corporal punishment for children! V-day was supposed to commemorate the brutal assassination of the Mirabal sisters in the Dominican Republic but She could not prevent

---

1   A reference, of course, to the English title of Bertrand Tavernier's 1980 film, *La mort en direct*, which was shot in Glasgow.

herself from thinking of Glasgow-born Ian Brady who insisted that 'Rape is not a crime, it is a state of mind. Murder is a hobby and a supreme pleasure'. How many Moors murderers were today on the square? She felt isolated from everyone, alienated from life. For her all earth was one thought and that was death. Death just hovering and wanting to claim his prey.

She had once entertained the idea of spending time in different pubs. She had hummed her way to the closest whisky bar, but now She did not know why. Drinking would in fact impair her vigilance, leave her open to trouble. So She decided to seek solace in the normality of daily chores. No ordinary person would be attacked, punished for living the most ordinary life. One had to be special, to do extraordinary deeds to be chosen. Doing the same thing every day at the same time would allow her to detect minute changes. She walked the same itinerary every day, took the same bus at exactly the same time, kept an eye on everyone. She took refuge in a dusty, drab, cold office high up in a tower. Safe for a while, She could gather strange and beautiful fruits to concoct her famous recipes. From the upper level. Sister Ann would be able to tell if the path was becoming bloody or if one could still see the lush greenery of the primal forest.

When she had fixed her choice on Scotland, she reckoned that it would be impossible to be in danger there. It was such an exotic place, with its haunted castles, its supernatural lakes, its moors, its seas that She, an anonymous person, could not fail to go unnoticed. She had set up home in a quiet neighbourhood, close to the Botanic Gardens. From her window She could see the Kibble Palace where everything was order and beauty, voluptuousness and luxury. But She knew it was a bad omen when She learnt that the Palace had been closed for repairs and that the rose garden was out of season. Walking into the garden could not bring back the splendour in the grass, the glory in the flowers.

Plus there was that wandering path leading down to the River Kelvin, its nightly crowds, its bizarre incidents. At night She could hear the raucous voices, the cracks and growls, the roars and howling. Screams were lost in the darkness of the night. Red was then the river's colour.

Her hope of going unnoticed was crushed the day she was to go to Edinburgh. She knew before opening the door. It was as if she had been attacked by thousands of glass particles, her whole body was frigid with fear and pain. She was being stalked by the unknown. On her way to Central Station, she could not recognise the people riding on bus number 90. She was being followed. She could hear the clanging of boots behind her. Her follower wanted her to know someone was there, not far away from her, able to hurt her anytime. She could smell the odour of death, could hear a rasping breathing like a child crying, but every time She bolted around she could not make sense of what she saw. There were flashes of red, of blood. Would She be able to prevent mayhem?

She could not go to the police nor to the Department of Forensic Sciences with her story of a red cape and iron boots. Sherlock Holmes himself would have found her weird and unbelievable, not to mention Inspector Puzzle from Edinburgh or whatever his name was. Any detective would pronounce her hysterical, histrionic. She could not rely on the authorities to find the right solutions.

She walked in the streets seeing so many deaths. The business and shopping streets were the place of all sorts of dangers. She had been warned not to carry her money with her but that was the least of her worries. She could see all those women attacked, raped and murdered. She heard their names and a date whispered in her ear: Diane McInally (1991), Karen McGregor (1993), Leona McGovern (1995), Marjorie Roberts (1995), Jackie Gallacher (1996), Tracy Wylde (1997), Margo Lafferty (1998). What would She have in common with these women? Why did someone recite those names to her as if it was a poem, a litany? She was also told about Bloody Mary and her husband Darnley who died in an explosion plotted by his wife in 1567. People talked about missing girls kidnapped, raped, killed with the complicity of their teacher, of improprieties by members of the royal families. All this was supposed to have a personal meaning but all those names made too much noise in her head for her to function properly.

Came the time she did not dare to wander in the town anymore. She would go to her tower, spend the day buried in her books. She would take a bus back to her lodgings early in the afternoon, stop at the Botanic Gardens and go to the nearest supermarket to buy herself the same salad bowl, the same sandwich and the same dessert. She would eat her daily treats in her room drinking piping-hot tea and watching 'Easterners'. She knew the threat was real but could not fathom why she was the only one to see it, to understand the dangers.

Unable to unravel the mysteries by herself She called her friend Suzanne to the rescue. It was for her friend the perfect occasion to drop work, husband and family commitments. Suzanne packed a suitcase. Without hesitation, she left Switzerland and the beloved mountains to take a plane in Geneva, land in London and arrive by the last flight at Glasgow airport. Suzanne was no Doctor Scarpetta, no Kathy Reichs but she knew a lot about human nature and understood her friend to be in troubled waters.

The next day, a phone call was made. They were to see in the late evening two fat ladies who would feed them information. The odd hour, the dreary weather sent them back to the Big Sleep. The streets were shiny with rain. The lights were bleak. They hopped into a cruising taxi on Great Western Road and asked the chauffeur to take them to Dumbarton Road. They entered number eighty-eight. It was a small, dim, smoky place. A place where you expected gangsters, spies to do their business unnoticed but it was full of families and happy-looking couples. Had they made a mistake? Misunderstood the instructions? They were told that nobody was expecting them, that no phone call had ever been made. They should try their luck somewhere else as they were not welcome there. Suzanne could not believe it, she had been in the room with her friend at the time of the phone call and knew what She had said. She thought of the different possibilities: the phone call had been misplaced. Was a wrong number. A joke. A more mysterious charade. A ploy to get them out. A sinister omen. She's conduct showed she was stressed and frightened but it did not look like the beginning of depression, she showed no sign of paranoia. But who would want to harm her? She was unknown in Glasgow, hadn't had time to make friends or enemies. Tomorrow Suzanne would slip out to go to the police but now was time to leave the place as she, too, could feel the hostility, the malevolence of the people there.

Out they went again in the dark streets of town. No taxi, only the sound of iron boots on the pavement. Run, said the wind. Run, said the moon. The two friends started to run but Suzanne could not keep up the pace. They ran up Argyle Street into Kelvingrove Park where each tree seemed to reach its limbs to hang them, each shrub to attack them. Out of breath, Suzanne begged her friend to slow down, to keep things in perspective. They had run without thinking and they were going around and around Park Circus. If She read the street signs She would see that they entered Park Terrace to go into Woodlands Terrace into Lynedoch Place, Park Quadrant and around again. So they stopped and wandered through Woodlands Road, Gibson Street to arrive quite by chance in Ashton Lane. There, hungry and cold, they found a place to restore themselves. Sitting in a courtyard in the mist of a hanging garden, they regaled themselves with luscious Orkney Organic Salmon, Lime and Vanilla Mash, an Intense Red Pepper and Vermouth Sauce and Salmon Beignet. After such a dinner they were ready to taste the local water. Suzanne was an adept of soft, almost tasteless water while She like the smoky or salty taste of local waters. They decided to try the Lagalvulin, the Ardbeg and the Laphroaig recommended by one of their informants. Strangely, this break in their investigation did not bring the disorder She had expected and they were able to walk back to their place without being followed by the Red Cape or his acolytes. So was it a vision or a waking dream?

Her confidence strengthened by the quietness of the night, Suzanne pleaded for a walking tour but She, still full of all the noise and fury of her preceding escapades, said that there was too much danger in the west of town. They had to solve the mysteries before Suzanne went back to work or else... They got on the number 90 bus and went to the end of the line. They passed the violent shopping and business streets, George Square and its Christmas village, the University of Strathclyde and its hill, to go beyond the city. Violence surely resided in the suburbs. They arrived in a place where all the clocks worked orange. Streets were deserted, clone houses lining street after street. Death was living there but its violence was not the kind threatening She. This was a violence of hoodlums, drunks and Skins. This was no future and despair. It was not the violence that was to invade her world. Glasgow had long been a breeding ground for gangs of criminals. Decades of poverty, unemployment, poor housing and macho culture cultivated in the pubs and shipyards had given a bad reputation to Glasgow so the authorities moved its troublemaking population out of the city in camp-like housing. Glasgow gangs, be they ice-cream gangs or others, attacked people near to them or those they disliked because they had foreign names or darker skin such as Iram Kahna who was murdered outside a chip shop or Kishwar Noor who was attacked by three white thugs. She and Suzanne were two white women, middle-aged going on older, they looked respectable but not rich and anyway they were not getting off the bus in the middle of nowhere.

There was nothing else to do but go back into the heart of town, to the centre of violence. They stopped at George Square, not to admire the Christmas spirit of the scene but to enter a one-time bank turned pub. Chatting with the natives, understanding the mood of the city, finding out if She's fears were founded would be easier in such a place. Strangers to local customs, it took them a while to get a table, order a pint of beer and some food. They were sitting next to two fat ladies. They rejoiced thinking that they had inverted the day and time of the rendezvous the night before. They struck up conversation with the two women to soon discover that they were not the two fat ladies in question. Nobody could tell them if and when death was going to strike. Maybe death was watching everyone but She was more sensitive to it than others. Maybe She was sick and should consult a doctor. Nobody else was hearing in their head names of murdered prostitutes. She reminded them of people who thrive on thrillers: her fear was a decoy, a screen for a too real violence.

But Suzanne's mind was not put at rest by these soothing words. She knew of The Nighthawk and his break-ins, of Peter Manuel who shot six people in two years, of the legendary Bible John, of Helen Puttock killed near Dumbarton Road, not far away from their missed rendezvous. They had talked of Marion Watt, Margaret Brown and their niece Vivienne, of Isabelle Cooke, of the Smart family. But most of all She had told her her reasons for not going to the police. She could not forget that Constable James Robertson had been arrested for the murder of his girlfriend. He had run her over several times with a stolen vehicle in Prospecthill Road. Nor could she forget that Howard Wilson was an ex-constable turned murderer.

She begged Suzanne to be careful: they had not been able to identify the enemy, to describe the threat; a bad move could bring them more danger. Suzanne should go back home as planned to put whoever was stalking She off the scent. Once Suzanne was gone, She would travel and try to lose her follower. She had planned a train trip to Bangor and was certain that nobody could keep up with her elaborate plan and complicated itinerary. Some officials knew she was in trouble and had given her instructions on how to reach them on their cellphone in case of dire need.

Suzanne was unhappy with this plan but she agreed to leave the next day. She had to go back to her work, her demanding husband, her never-ending obligations. Suzanne also had trust in universal justice, knew that there was somewhere a master plan and a benevolent creature. Work would be the best therapy to take her friend's mind off all those morbid events. The same advice was given at dinner by the friendly couple who had invited them. Suzanne asked them to keep an eye on She and to phone her if anything unusual happened.

Suzanne left the next morning trying to reassure herself that She would get better soon and that by the time She came back to Switzerland all her fears would have been alleviated. Could Bangor be as dangerous for her state of mind as Scotland had been or would she find a haven from her fears?

She went to Bangor, where the earth and the ocean meet. She did a lot of walking there, wandering in the town and near the sound, she knew that, despite what everyone said, she was being stalked, she was on death watch. She shook the dream from herself. There would be no beginning, no end, no red inferno. She would be transported to a world from which the bright sun would be extinguished. A black rain would fall, ice would be all around.

Nobody would strangle her, nobody would shoot her, cut her throat with a dagger. Life would slowly ebb from her. She would walk into a large pall of dark clouds which were fated to smother her. She would pass a woman with the West in her eyes who would bring the unreal world too strangely near her.

Silvia Ricci Lempen

That's me there on the Photo

Oxford, Wednesday 20 October 2004

My father died twenty years and one day ago. For several years, I never failed to remember that anniversary, then it was just every other year, then hardly ever. *Sic transit gloria patris*, we'll meet again on the Day of Judgement. But then yesterday, quite out of the blue, I once again became aware of the date because of all the emerald-coloured lawns, mown very short in parallel lines, which are to Oxford what the Sugar Loaf Mountain is to Rio. On his one and only trip to Britain, when he was already quite elderly, my father had been so fascinated by the lawns of the Oxford colleges that he took it into his head to create something similar in the garden of our house in Rome, where, during the summer, it is over 30 degrees and not a drop of rain falls for weeks on end. No need to add, of course, that in spite of turning the hosepipe on it for several hours a day at dawn and dusk, the colour of our lawn was always more akin to the yellow of D'Artagnan Senior's old nag than its lush Oxford counterparts. My father's plan not only failed, in fact the current occupants of the house in Rome wisely got rid of any vestiges of it by allowing their dogs to frolic on the lawn.

This morning I woke up thinking not really about my father, but more generally about the pointlessness of human activities and the following hours simply confirmed the appropriateness of this relativist mood. First of all, as I was eating the generous Breakfast which according to the terms and conditions came with my Bed, whilst at the same time taking some notes, a lady who was imposing and francophile in equal measure suggested that I shouldn't waste my life working. It was a funny way to start the day. Then, as I was visiting the Bodleian Library which houses 7,135,000 volumes, I fell to wondering if it was really wise to add to that number for future generations. Was it worth forcing that venerable institution to extend its 184 kilometres of shelves by a good thirty centimetres simply because of me? In short, everything came together in such a way that, by the beginning of the afternoon, I no longer had any illusions whatsoever about the importance of the mark I might leave on Earth.

Here I am then at the entrance to Christ Church College, aware of being a fleck of dust, destined to return to dust, no more nor less than Lewis Carroll or even Henry VIII. Unfortunately, the centre-piece of the visit, the Dining Hall, is closed today (I am not told why), which means I get in to the College for a reduced price. I take comfort in the thought that the most important thing is the atmosphere. As far as a guidebook goes, I am woefully under-equipped, since I only have the *Lonely Planet* guide to Great Britain, which has a lot more to say on youth hostels than on architecture and royal dynasties, but at the College entrance I was given an explanatory leaflet with numbers for each stage of the tour: 1. *The Meadow Building.* 2. *The Cloister* – up to that point, all is well, it's atmospheric, there's atmosphere in spades, in fact. Then it says 'turn your back to the medieval garden, go up the steps, left into the tower (3) where you will find a wide stone staircase.' It's the staircase which leads to the Dining Hall and at the foot of the staircase elastic strips confirm unfortunately that entry is forbidden. As I hesitate for a moment, toying with the idea of giving the museum keepers the slip and secretly going under the barrier (I am Swiss, but also Italian), my eyes light on what appears to be graffiti written in chalk on a kind of black service door. The meaning of the words – *No Peel* – escapes me completely, maybe it's the name of a rock band, but whatever it is I marvel at two things. Firstly, the fact that even at Christ Church College the students scrawl on public walls and secondly, the fact that the museum keepers, apparently won over to the cause of freedom of speech by an atavistic reflex since the time of the *Magna Carta*, have done absolutely nothing to repair forthwith the scandalous attack on this historic place. In fact, once I read point 3 in the leaflet, I learn that the graffiti is almost two centuries old: 'This was a protest against the Home Secretary, Sir Robert Peel (a Christ Church man!) who in 1829 proposed greater freedom for Catholics.'

Standing opposite the *Tom Tower* in the *Quad* (point 6), I gaze fixedly at the clock which is set at Oxford time, that is, five minutes later than Greenwich, and which used to ring out 101 strokes at 9 p.m., the curfew for students at the College. There must have been those who were coming back to work and those who used a variety of tricks to stay out of college enjoying themselves in brothels and bars. Did they get sent down if they were caught? The brochure doesn't say much, perhaps I can get some more information in the *Lonely Planet*. I flick through the guidebook. Nothing more on the *Quad*, but a whole paragraph on the words *'No Peel'*: 'This graffiti dates from the mid-seventeenth century, when the college doctor prescribed raw potato peels to counteract the effects of an outbreak of plague. The cure didn't work and the students, sick of their enforced diet, took a hot knife to wood.'

I look up to the *Quad*'s lawn which does indeed seem to me to be a bit less green than the others, maybe because of its size. And I say to myself that the terrible thing about human activities (writing a book, keeping a lawn in perfect condition or protesting about what is wrong with the world) is not so much that they often end in failure but that we can never even be sure they've been attempted.

Menai Bridge, Saturday 23 October

Three giggly young girls are climbing the path quickly, chatting, out of breath, you can hardly see them through the leaves, in the half-light of the dusk, but you can hear from far off their chorus of high voices. We are coming down the other way, towards the sea. Bad luck, P. has chosen to visit me on the first weekend of the autumn when it is raining hard, but in spite of everything I am keen to show him Church Island.

As we aren't speaking much, busy holding onto our umbrellas and avoiding slipping on the dead leaves, the girls don't notice us at first. Once they catch sight of us, their vague six-legged group moves in and out like an accordeon, laughingly shouting 'Sorry, sorry' and then comes to a halt. But what are they sorry about? We haven't heard anything, not even if they were speaking Welsh or English.

They must be fourteen, fifteen at the most, and contrary to expectations they are interested in us. The fact that we are foreigners, which they quickly deduced from our denials, not only makes them feel relieved but also fascinates them and there is genuine friendliness on their pale, childlike faces which are impressively toothy. 'Are you on holiday?' and of course 'Where do you come from?' What's more, I get the feeling they consider us to be very old, at least as old as their great-grandparents, perhaps because of our plan to go over to the island just when the entire village is heading to the fair. They are wearing low-waisted jeans, lowcut T-shirts and on top either a short-sleeved checked shirt or a leather waistcoat with laces. We laugh, embarrassed, astonished by their bare goose-pimpled arms streaked with rain. They must like chewing those artificial sweets which look like acid green or strawberry pink spaghetti. We tell them to have a good time: 'Enjoy the fair!'

Church Island is linked to the mainland by a short stretch of land which you can walk along and on either side of it you can see a layer of mud as flat as if a steamroller had passed over it, due to the ebb and flow of the tide. We walk around the little island which is tiny and, apart from the Church of Saint Tysilio, entirely occupied by a cemetery; there is still just enough light to make out the inscriptions on the slate tombstones. We are quite alone. To please me, P. says it's a lovely view even though the rain, which is falling harder and harder, is making it difficult to see the Strait.

Later that evening we go back to the village where the fair is in full swing, despite the downpour. People have come from Bangor and from all over Anglesey, leaving their cars and vans (*Wedding Cakes and Confectioners, One-Hour Photo Lab, www. adventure-angling.uk, Bull's Head Inn*) absolutely anywhere by the side of the main road from Holyhead or by the side of the narrower one from Beaumaris. I say something about the lack of signposted carparks, which would be organised by the police in Switzerland, and P. replies that since no-one is losing their temper they must think their system is better. Thousands of feet are pounding the wet asphalt where the yellow and red lights of the attractions are reflected – *Kamikaze, Banzaï, Vortex, Loop on the Top* – boom boom boom goes the ubiquitous heart of the fair. There's a smell of rubber, of fireworks, of wet hair, a stale smell of fried cod on acrylic jumpers. I was told that the fair people settle in Menai Bridge every year at the same period, the last weekend in October, which is less odd here than in a southern country for, as I learned in *The Rough Guide to Wales*: 'The bottom line is that it's impossible to say with any degree of certitude that the weather will be pleasant in any given month.' Whatever the truth of the matter may be, the food stand which has the most customers is the one selling Italian ice-cream. It is decorated with a realistic painting of an ice-cream which has three different flavours and evokes the heat of a late afternoon in Rimini. Edible versions of this archetypal ice-cream cornet are being carried around like church candles by hundreds of people and the rain carves tiny tracks down the ice-cream.

I think again about the three giggly young girls we saw earlier. I'd like to see them again, give them a little wave of recognition, but how can I possibly find them amongst all these other girls who look just like them, all in six-legged groups, laughing into each other's shoulders, or holding tight to one other, shrieking, as they are launched into the rust-coloured sky on fair wheels or rush by into ecstasy or forgetfulness in carriages on vertical metal rails. They shriek, as do the lads, but you hear them less, perhaps because shrieking is a girl thing, perhaps because male voices are deeper and stand out less against the hammer blow of techno music. I must have yelled like that myself, in another life, on the Big Dipper in a fairground, but the sound seems very far away from me, as painful as things you've never experienced, yells in English where all the vowels are mixed up, yells emerging from mouths which are full of rain – I can feel that my feet are wet and they're right, I've got old.

Belfast, Thursday 28 October

The first story in Alice Munro's book *Open Secrets*,[1] which is called 'Carried Away', tells the story of Louisa, a librarian in the municipal library in the fictional town of Carstairs, Ontario. One day in February 1917 Louisa receives a letter from a young man she doesn't remember but who claims he was a regular user of the library before being sent to Europe as a soldier. Jack is now in a military hospital on the front and is once again thinking about the young woman whose name he doesn't even know (the letter is addressed to 'the Carstairs librarian') and to whom he has never spoken. An increasingly intimate exchange of letters then ensues. However, at the end of the war, when Jack returns to Carstairs, he doesn't try to meet Louisa, who learns through the local newspaper that he has married another woman. He dies in a work accident a few years later without Louisa ever having seen him face to face.

I bought this book in Oxford last week, but as I was reading another one at the time I only started it at Liverpool Airport, as I was waiting for my Easyjet flight to Belfast. It's the kind of book which opens up valves on every square inch of my body and through these valves I suddenly start to breathe differently, profoundly, totally. Just thinking that there is someone who was capable of writing such a book makes me feel that it is right to put up with everything – the

1   Vintage, 1995.

close combat with language, the feeling of solitude, the quarrels with editors, the unpleasantness of critics – in return for the privilege of trying to write literature. Since my arrival, however, I've made little progress with it for in Belfast my attention was required for a thousand things, involving the university, food and, of course, the botanic gardens.

Yesterday afternoon I had two hours to kill which I would have liked to spend with Alice Munro but when I went back to my hotel after lunch I noticed that my room hadn't yet been cleaned. My discussion with the receptionist about this was neither short nor entirely clear, my comprehension of Belfast English being subject to what is known in the pharmaceutical world as 'delayed action'. In any case, I was led into a small lounge where I was asked to wait for an indeterminate length of time. Unfortunately, I didn't have *Open Secrets* with me and I didn't dare go back up to get it so as not to look like I was pressurising a manual worker, the chambermaid, who doubtless was more in need of a rest than me.

In the little lounge with its stuffy atmosphere and armchairs with green covers and flounces, I spied a shelf with classical works on it. I took one of them, an old edition of Keats's first collection of poems, which struck me as so difficult that I went for the easy option and read the preface. So I learned that when it came out in 1817, the work had been so badly received that some of the very few people who bought it returned it to the bookshop, demanding their money back. In a letter to Keats's brother, the publishers wrote, with an elegant sense of understatement: *'We regret that your brother even requested us to publish his book, or that our opinion of his talent should have led us to acquiesce in undertaking it.'*

The British have understatement, the Swiss have *Schadenfreude*, the usefulness of which, when an author needs consolation at not having sold many books, is well-known. But I can confirm, with a certain sense of satisfaction, that the account of Keats's failure only evoked in me a superficial rejoicing and had no effect whatsoever on the rate of my breathing.

I am sitting on a bench outside the Europa Bus Station in Belfast, opposite the bay from which the bus for the airport leaves and I'm still reading the short story 'Carried Away'. Buses are constantly arriving on the forecourt, turning, parking, filling up with passengers and leaving again for different destinations whose names (apart from Londonderry, because of the clashes between Catholics and Protestants) are all completely unknown to me. I've been here a little under two days and I've learned nothing about this little bit of the island. The people are just like they are everywhere, dressed in cheap jackets, eating cress, cheese and mayonnaise sandwiches, carrying plastic bags, they look tired. Maybe the hotel chambermaid arrived here this morning at the crack of dawn and is at this moment in a bus taking her home to Castlereagh, Portadown or Ballymena.

But it's strange; in the short story I'm reading there's also something about a bus station in a town about a hundred kilometres from Carstairs, where Louisa, who is now an elderly widow, is waiting on a warm summer afternoon for the six o'clock bus which will take her home after a medical appointment. It's now the mid-1950s. Different things have happened in Louisa's life, and yet at the same time nothing really remarkable has happened, except for Jack who is dead but not dead, since for her he's never really been alive – a normal life, she says to the man who has sat down next to her on one of the makeshift old chairs in the bus station, for in fact it's a temporary one, not the one Louisa usually uses, which is being renovated. It's a place which is suspended between the past and the present, between strangeness and reality. 'I don't recognise you', Louisa first of all said to the man when he spoke to her. And he replied: 'Well, no. I guess not. Of course, you wouldn't.'

Here's the bus for the airport, everyone leaps into action. I get in mechanically, thinking about something else – the fantastical encounter between Jack and Louisa, delayed by thirty years, Jack wearing a yellow shirt and not looking at all like a ghost. That can happen in all the bus stations in the world, there just has to be someone to invent it.

London, Sunday 31 October

No, I'm not going to have a quick one at the window, even if I'm pretty sure that the smell would drift away and no-one would notice it. I'm exhausted after a journey from Bangor to London at the tender mercy of the privatised railways, the defining characteristic of a Virgin train being to be delayed and to have reserved seats without any visible numbers. What's more, when I arrived in Euston, I felt like I was in a remake of the scene described in *Therapy*, a novel by David Lodge published almost ten years ago: in order to get from where the trains arrive to the taxis on the lower level, you have to go down quite a long staircase, dragging your suitcase (although it's true that you can stop for a rest on each step, since the queue goes all the way up the staircase). Anyway, now that I've arrived safe and sound, I'd like nothing more than to lie down on the bed with two cushions under my head and smoke a cigarette as I watch something mind-numbing on the television. But on the papers I was given at the reception it says that the residence is non-smoking, completely non-smoking, and there is such a prim atmosphere in the place that I dare not disobey the rules. I get dressed again, put on my shoes and go to smoke outside, walking up and down Mecklenburgh Square.

Mecklenburgh Square is a theatre without a play. Nobody. Nighttime reflections of the white columns, the copper plates, the black varnished doors. The polished plates of austere-looking offices, which are not to be frequented by just anyone; doors which are destined to open rarely, with a brief, discreet buzzing. For a time Virginia and Leonard Woolf set up their Hogarth Press in one of these buildings. The middle of the square is occupied by a garden surrounded by a railing covered in climbing plants. The gate is locked. I could ask for the key, for I also read in the papers given to me that the guests in my residence, visiting writers and academics, have exclusive use of the garden; as it happens, this privilege doesn't much tempt me on this cold Halloween weekend.

I walk along by the garden railing. Most of the houses are dark or weakly lit but on the second floor of one of them there must be a reception going on: window ajar, shadowy figures, discreet noises floating out, slicing through the silence of the square. I stay there for a moment, my eyes raised, imagining the atmosphere in a reception on a Sunday evening in Bloomsbury.

The sound of high heels. A woman hurries along, puffing on her cigarette. Shiny hair, as bright as metal, long open coat, very short dress, fishnet stockings. She is smoking with one hand whilst with the other clutching to her chest a tiny evening bag. She must have got out of a taxi which she asked to stop some distance away so that she could at least have a quick drag. She looks a bit suspiciously at this other smoker leaning against the garden railing – what bad luck, she's late and now she's been caught red-handed in shameful company with another addict. Forced to speak to her when, in a little while, they will meet again over a glass of champagne in the crystal-clear atmosphere of the reception. Fortunately, after having a quick look she is reassured, the pest is wearing boots and a mackintosh, togged out like that she's unlikely to also be one of the guests. She puts out her cigarette butt with her shoe. I turn my back on her, so as not to intrude on the recomposition of her social face, without a single mark of vice, before she rings the doorbell.

Mecklenburgh Square, 31 October, a quarter to nine in the evening. I'm going to go back in, there's nothing more to see. There is though, another human being has emerged from the depths and is standing, not immobile, but without moving forward, about four or five yards in front of me, at the edge of the pavement; a speaking human, since mumbling, which disturbs the silence, is emerging from him, as well as a noise of – no, it must be something else, I can't believe that this sound of running water, like a hosepipe on the pavement – his right shoulder hunched, his head bent to the ground, a fumbling to close his flies. He hears me approach, straightens up, turns round and shouts 'Sorry darling!' in a horribly familiar voice which sounds nothing like the voice of a Head of

Department introducing a cultural talk or the voice of a fussy porter at the desk of an academic residence.

I struggle to find a witticism which will put this oaf in his place, but the task is beyond me in English and instead of looking daggers at him, I get the feeling I look more like an old bag. And yet the guy, turned into a bit of a show-off by my silence, actually goes to approach me. The residence is thirty paces away on the opposite side of the road, I am practically running when I cross the threshold, pursued by a cheeky voice which rings out over the night-time desert of Mecklenburgh Square: 'Keep smiling darling, keep smiling!'

Glasgow, Thursday 4 November 2004

In the fairy tale there was something you weren't meant to think about (I forget what) as you were digging under the oak tree since not thinking about it was the only way of finding the treasure. Of course, it's impossible, the ties which are formed in the brain are stronger than a convict's chains. Psychoanalysis tells us that in dreams two terms often come together as one; so it's possible that once I'm back in Switzerland I might dream that John Kerry, reduced to half his normal height, was driving a bus in Glasgow in the land of giants.

It's eight o'clock in the morning and I've just returned from breakfast which I ate in silence alongside people from a variety of Asian countries who are attending a conference. As I wait for it to be time to leave, I watch on television the speeches by the loser and winner of the American presidential election. This event of global significance in fact has absolutely nothing to do with the reasons why, on 4 November, I am here on the sixth floor of a building on Cathedral Street surrounded by such a volume of air that it feels as if I could fly out the window. And yet I get the feeling that in a year from now if someone asks me if I've ever been to Glasgow, the first thing I'll say is that I was there precisely on the day when Kerry's defeat

in the American presidential election of 2004 was announced. It's
the same with Hamburg, where I stayed for a month in September
2001: if someone asks me about that city I say, just think, on the
afternoon of the 11 September I was walking in the Hanseviertel,
the commercial centre of the city, and it was there in the window
of a television shop that I saw the towers fall for the first time.
But there's something else, the links in the chain, the feelings, the
fragments of ideas (that's very often what also holds the dream together). What are people saying, I can't understand them, if only
my German were a bit better, all I can see is that they've put their
umbrellas down because we're in a shopping mall but they're holding
them so casually that they're dripping inside their shoes, which appears to indicate a certain emotion, confusion or hushed excitement.
But the remarks exchanged, in fact discreet and full of Hanseatic
reserve, form an impenetrable verbal hide, making any hypothesis
at all entirely possible. For example: it's the phase which is known
as 'teasing' in a brand new advertising campaign, which is why we don't
know what the product is. Or: flying a plane into the Twin Towers is
the virtual challenge of the week in a very popular German television
gameshow which is on every Tuesday afternoon at four o'clock. The
links in the chain which ensure its continuity; I told myself it was a
local custom, which didn't particularly shock the locals. That in fact
is my real memory.

I'm sitting in a room in Glasgow filing my nails as I watch the
television. The window is behind me but what can be seen through
the window, an unusually big sky and a view of the urban landscape,
is part of the moment just as much as what is happening on the
screen. Mountains of stones, as wide as they are high, massive towers
which have purple lights around them at night – which is what I
saw the day before yesterday in the early evening as I was arriving on
the bus from the airport. So, without opening it, I abandoned my
suitcase in my room and, forgetting my purely sociological plan of
starting my exploration of the city in a pub, I began to walk with no
particular route in mind, until night fell, amongst these earthbound

liners whose outlines faded into the dark. I walked and walked and as I did so I could feel myself growing, like Alice in Wonderland, I could feel myself get stronger, expanding into the space, taking over all that vastness rather than being crushed by it and made to feel small. I thought to myself, this is a city where you forget to be afraid. It was new for me, big is beautiful, a major discovery when you are 1 metre 55 tall – but in this instance it was my spirit which was affected.

I watch the speeches given by the loser and the winner of the American presidential election. I already know what to expect regarding the results, because last night, unwilling to make any effort whatsoever on the gastronomic front, instead of going for a meal I watched the BBC whilst eating a Sainsbury's salad which came with a smidgen of sauce. I'm not interested in the winner, we're in for another four years and in the near future there'll be plenty of opportunities to admire his loquacity. The loser says why, even if he's lost, he still has complete trust in God and the Nation. I can see he's lying: he's in despair, his long face looks more horsey than ever and he'd love to slap his adversary's chubby face, roll on the ground yelling, cry his heart out in the arms of his mother or his analyst. I can see that his height cannot prevent him from feeling small, small inside, ashamed and pitiful. I can also see that he thinks that the worst torture of all is having to put on a good show and pretend to be tall.

Translated by Joy Charnley

Donal McLaughlin

Mitbringsel

In 2004, Donal McLaughlin spent six months in Bern as its first 'Scottish Writing Fellow' in a new exchange between the Swiss capital and the City of Glasgow. The residency attracted him both as a writer and as a translator and his contribution to this volume reflects this. The Bern exchange, together with a return visit to Switzerland in 2005 to attend the Solothurn Literary Festival, led him to begin translating three Swiss writers: Franco Supino, Clo Duri Bezzola and Pedro Lenz. It is his hope that the hitherto unpublished translations included here will help to interest potential funders and publishers in these very fine writers. His own writing is represented by an extract from a book, currently in progress, inspired by a long-distance walk around part of Lake Lucerne. He regards all four projects as 'Mitbringsel' – not souvenirs as such, but things he has brought back from Switzerland; for others, as much as for himself.[1]

Franco Supino

Ciao amore, ciao (2004) is the fourth novel to be published by Franco Supino (born 1965). The son of Italian immigrants to Switzerland, Supino writes in German. *Ciao amore, ciao* is based on the lives of two real-life singers, the Egyptian-born diva Dalida (1934–1987) and the Italian *cantautore* Luigi Tenco (1938–1967). It is well known that Dalida and Tenco competed at Sanremo in 1967 with a song composed

---

1   A fifth project, an 80-page book, has already reached fruition: Donal McLaughlin, *The Artist's Residence* (Bern: Edition Ensuite, 2005).

by the protest singer Tenco and that their exit in the qualifying rounds led to Tenco's suicide. Supino's version of this story, with its central characters of Iolanda and Gigi Mai, reflects the failure of the entertainment industry in the late 1960s to respond to the pressing issues of the period, not least to the emerging culture of protest. In the chapter presented here, the two musicians meet for the first time.

Chapter 16

The bar stood back from the pavement on the opposite side of the street, the sun slanted down on three old plane trees, beneath which a few small tables and odd chairs stood around, in no particular order. Iolanda and Elli stepped out of the building – right into the dry heat. Rome was eerily quiet, like a ghost town. Those who hadn't left town were hiding from the afternoon sun in whatever shade they could find.

Inside, at the bar, some of the staff from IMG were standing, sipping at their iced coffees or glasses of white wine. The light made the wine look green. Doriani was sitting with Luigi at a small table. Elli headed towards them, grabbed two chairs, and pushed them towards the table.

'May I introduce you?' Doriani said to Iolanda. 'Luigi Mai, known as Gigi. He, too, is contracted to us. A very promising *cantautore* who's already written some wonderful songs.'

Luigi had been sitting with his back to the door. He turned in slow motion and examined her face, her eyes. She had removed her white sunglasses with the huge lenses, meanwhile. Her reddish hair didn't go well with her brown eyes and eyebrows. The lines of her face were delicately drawn. With each passing second, any nervousness was vanishing. Before him, he saw a grown woman – with only the slightest hint of a girl. He no longer felt agitated, that tension now replaced by self-confident curiosity.

'What kind of songs do you compose?'

The first thing Iolanda's mother always wanted to know, if Iolanda told her about a man, was: 'È bello?' – 'Is he handsome?'

'Yes, Mamma, he's handsome. Dark eyes, thick eyebrows, a good head of hair, strong features, nice hands. What else? As for his clothing, he's one of these young intellectuals, have you heard about them – the Existentialist philosophers, with their black turtlenecks and jackets? He doesn't come across as arrogant, though – he can even look at you in a shy kind of way. There's something simple, down-to-earth, in the way he responds to people. I think he's a country boy. What age might he be? Younger than me, for sure'.

Iolanda looked at him. He was slim. When he stood up to greet someone, his ribs showed through his thin black pullover.

Doriani and Elli were talking. They took turns at speaking to Luigi. The subject was Iolanda, her forthcoming projects, and how IMG saw her future in Italy.

Iolanda wasn't paying attention, but smoking. She answered if someone asked her something, about some appearance of hers, or other. With Duke Wellington, in Berlin, yes – when was that again?

Luigi didn't say a word, he wasn't paying attention either, but smoking, and he was struggling to hide his impatience with what Elli and Doriani were saying.

If you see her sitting here like this, he thought, she comes across as being reticent; insecure, almost. She lets these men speak for her, doesn't contradict them, nods politely from time to time, looks as bored and embarrassed as a teenager whose parents are boasting to distant relatives about her good marks at school.

He looked at her. She returned his gaze.

'Do you live in Rome, signore?' she asked.

'I do – and I have to go now ...' To the amazement of Doriani and Elli, Luigi stood up. 'Would you like a lift, signora? May I drive you to your hotel?'

'I was planning to hail a taxi ...'

'My Vespa is just outside,' Luigi said. 'As you've probably noticed: everything here is a set-up, people very much wanted me to meet you... So allow me to take this opportunity to warn you against me.'

That was the reason for Elli's allusion earlier to the repertoire that needs changing, Iolanda thought. She looked at Elli, took him by the shoulder, and stood up. He winced. He obviously wasn't accustomed to being touched by women. Iolanda's mood had improved in an instant for it now looked as if she wouldn't have to spend the evening in a dull hotel, or in the tiresome company of producers desperate for recognition.

Luigi suggested showing her some of the sights of Rome. She accepted, gratefully. 'I visit many cities, but only rarely do I manage to look at one.' She could just as well have said: I am on the road so much, I'm on a different stage every night, I have no private life, I never get to go out with someone. Today is an exception.

'And then we'll go for something to eat. What do you say to pizza?'

'Pizza is always good.'

He asked her to sit on the pillion, then started the engine. He's not as impenetrable as he seemed in the bar, she thought to herself, relieved.

Luigi took her to her hotel. Iolanda wanted to freshen up and change her clothes. He waited for her at the entrance, checking out the clientele of one of Rome's best addresses. The world belongs to that lot, he told himself.

Iolanda emerged from the door, opened for her by a pageboy in the way he'd been trained. She was now wearing a simple, bright skirt, made of that high-quality Egyptian cotton with which her mother had worked in Shubra.

'What are you looking at me like that for? Don't you like what I'm wearing, signore?'

'Why have you dressed like a student, signora? Do you wish to look younger?'

Idiot, Iolanda thought. She looked him in the eye.

Did he want to provoke or insult her? He had really beautiful eyes and they were looking at her calmly and innocently.

'It suits you very well, signora,' Luigi said and he turned his engine on. 'Climb aboard, why don't you.'

Iolanda climbed on behind him. 'What you're planning seems somehow familiar,' she yelled, laughing, into his ear. 'Mr Gregory Peck!'

And he replied: 'You, too, are on a Roman holiday - and I, I intend to use you for my own purposes.'

Luigi drove in the dusk from one Roman sight to the next, Iolanda's dress flapped against her ankles, the wind blew through her hair, her arms hugged Luigi, holding her tight against his body. It had been a long time since she had hugged a man like this, simply to hold on. The Vespa stuttered across the cobbles. Luigi tooted the horn. Everywhere, now, were people and vehicles: suddenly, with the cooler time of day, everyone had crawled out of their catacombs and caves and was now flooding every alleyway and street, be it on foot, by bike or by car, suddenly the fountains were flowing again, soon the streetlights would be turned on, people were calling out, sitting, discussing, gesticulating, kissing each other and walking hand-in-hand, were playing football, sitting halfway up or down staircases and in the cafés.

Finally, Luigi rolled across Piazza Navona and came to a stop before the fountain. 'Shall we sit here for a while?'

Iolanda climbed off the Vespa.

She was dizzy, perhaps from being shaken around, perhaps because she'd eaten nothing all day, perhaps because she was exhausted. Together, they sat down on the wall at the edge of the fountain. Blinking into the evening sun, Iolanda said: 'That was exactly the way I always imagined Italy to be when I was young.'

'Are you here for the first time, signora?'

No. This Spring she had also stood here, at this fountain, when her brother had got married. 'No, no. He lives, as the whole family does, in Paris. But nothing else would do: they wanted to get married in Rome. My sister-in-law is Italian.' She'd been assured even then that Piazza Navona was one of the most atmospheric in Rome. 'Fair enough,' she said, looking into Luigi's eyes, 'but it's not all down to the Square.'

The water splashing down filled the air with spray which glistened in the dusk before the facade of Sant'Agnese.

Luigi was now explaining: one of the figures on the fountain, as a precaution, is raising a hand towards the church, as if to prevent it from collapsing. The other figure has its head covered – so as not to have to see the mistakes the builders made. Jibes made by Bernini, who built the fountain, against his rival, the church architect, Borromini.

'I know that story.'

'But, of course. Rome has only anecdotes which everyone already knows.'

Iolanda laughed cheekily.

'You are not laughing at my joke, signora. You are laughing at me. – Do I have to throw you into the fountain?' Luigi grabbed her beneath the arms. She screamed but didn't jump away. 'Where would you like to land, signora? Which is your favourite river god: the Ganges, the Plate, the Danube or the Nile?'

'The Nile, of course.'

'The Nile is the one with his eyes covered.' He laid his hands across her eyes. And she allowed him to.

When Luigi removed his hands, he saw the tears in her eyes. He was astonished. Asked her what was wrong.

'Nothing,' she said. 'It's not because of you, signore.'

After the meal they strolled along the Tiber, hand-in-hand. Luigi asked Iolanda how come she spoke Italian so well.

For a while they walked together in silence.

'Tell me about your childhood, Iolanda,' Luigi suddenly said. 'That interests me. Did you do all your schooling in Italian?'

He stopped. 'Come on – let's sit down.' A staircase led to a jetty at which boats were moored. They sat on the top step. Iolanda crossed one leg over the other, supporting herself to the side with her left hand. Luigi was holding her right. He closed her fingers in against her palm, before then taking her thumb with his other hand.

'What kind of game's this?' Iolanda asked, laughing. 'This little piggy?'

'Something like that. Tell me, which smells from Shubra do you remember?'

Iolanda laughed again and shook her hair gently. He leaned closer, looking firmly into her eyes.

'Curry?'

Without looking, he opened out her index finger. 'What colour do you think of when you think of Shubra?'

'White. No, wait – ochre is better.'

'What were you most afraid of as a child?'

'The dark.'

'If you could be a child again, what would you like to have that you didn't have before?'

'A father.'

'What is your mother's greatest desire?'

'To be a grandmother.'

By now, her whole hand was open. He looked away from her eyes and down at her palm. Then, with his index finger, he traced the lines he found there. Iolanda looked across his black mop of hair towards the water. She was amazed at the piety with which he could perform these actions. A shiver went through her and she shuddered.

'Now it's your turn, Luigi,' she said as he sat up again. Iolanda had taken his hand and placed her palm on his.

'Smell?'

'That of wine fermenting.'

'Colour?'

'Ochre is good.'

'What were you afraid of as a child?'

'Even nowadays, I still can't sleep without a light on. – And I would also have liked to have a father. – And my mother would also like to be a grandmother.'

Iolanda sat up again and raised her hands, he did the same and their palms pressed together, lightly. 'One perfect match after another,' Iolanda said.

They kissed. Until a boat passed by. Some wild teenagers aboard it tried to spray them with water.

Iolanda waved to them.

'I grew up on a remote farm,' Luigi told her. 'Imagine a hilly landscape, hot in the summer, foggy in winter. And suddenly I had to leave there and live in a house above a severe drop to the sea.'

(Translated by Donal McLaughlin
from: Franco Supino, *Ciao amore, ciao*
(Zürich: Rotpunktverlag, 2004))

Clo Duri Bezzola

Clo Duri Bezzola (1945-2004) was a prize-winning poet, born in Scuol/Graubünden, who wrote in Romansh and German. The author of various volumes of prose and poetry in Romansh, Bezzola is also known for his novel *Zwischenzeit* (Pendo: 1996). The poems here are taken from the bilingual volume *Das gestohlene Blau / Il blau engulà*.

DAWN

Your breath
caresses me
from slumber

I put my ear
to your heart

Beneath your skin
stories
start to stir

REFLECTION

Tonight
you are like the moon

Offer me
a crescent of skin
and turn
to the stars
In my shadow
the sun
caresses you

GENTLY

My hand
has run over
your skin
smells of mushroom
and cinnamon
My tongue
still shies
the light

SKETCH

A dream
has made it
under your skin

Has painted
frost patterns
on it

LOOKING BACK

A face I do not know
has strewn
flowers
across my path

I turn
towards you
the bouquet is
for you

AXIOM

There is
no difference
between
the mountains
and
the sea

Just their
common
proximity
to the sky

RACE

the sky
frozen
mirrors
a land
of snow

between the two
the birds play
at who can get away
first
and back again

MEGALOMANIA

In free-fall
gulls sieve
the air,
peck the blue
from the sea
as a gift
for the sky

Tomorrow,
we'll get our revenge
the fish swear

THE TIME IT TAKES

We hesitate
like the wind
and the clouds
between coming
and going

Wait
for the sky
to regale us
with its stolen blue

(Translated by Donal McLaughlin
from Clo Duri Bezzola, *Das gestohlene Blau /
Il blau engulà* (Zürich: Pendo Verlag, 1998))

Pedro Lenz

Pedro Lenz (born 1965) is best known for his poems *Die Welt ist ein Taschentuch* (Bern: X-Time, 2002) and, more recently, a hilarious fake guide to Swiss provincial literature, *Das Kleine Lexikon der Provinzliteratur* (Zürich: bilgerverlag, 2005). A brilliant performer of his work – as proven by Poetry Slam successes and fast-selling CDs – Lenz spent six months in Glasgow in 2005 as the first Swiss writer to benefit from the new exchange with Bern. The translations presented here were performed at various bilingual readings during that residency.

YA EEJIT, FRANZ

Suddenly,
on the way home we were,
you started on about her.

And by the time we knew
that she has fine
white skin, and that
her breasts are small and beautiful,
by the time we'd learned
that sometimes, afterwards,
she has to cry,
but just silently and
just a wee bit, like,
by the time we knew all that,
you'd reached the point
you'd lost her.

That right, Franz?
Ya eejit, Franz? You now know
you should've kept
your mouth shut.

TRANSIT

In my memory it's as if
it was always winter,
all those years, only ever winter.
We drove to work.
It was always still dark.
The lorry had two
benches at the back.
We sat opposite one another,
leaning forward,
our lower arms resting
on our knees.
I was the youngest,
listened to them saying nothing,
saying nowt myself.
I've forgotten
their faces.
Can just see
their hands, all those strong,
still hands.
Some were holding fags
or flasks
or sandwiches, all wrapped-up.
Others were just hingin there, empty.
That was all I could see:
twelve or fourteen hands.
And mostly I wished
the journey would last forever,
forever and ever,
in those two rows of seats
in an old Ford Transit.

THE TENANT

Once,
to give you an example,
he planted onions.
At some point, later,
he had to give
the garden up.
The piece of land
behind the flats
was tarmacked over.

Now he has
a parking space
with yellow lines round it.
Every Saturday,
he sweeps his space clean
with a brush.

If his son were ever to visit,
he'd appreciate
this dedicated parking space.

DOG NIGHTS

Nando, it was, told us,
a local.

From up there,
from the lighthouse
at Santander,
from the cliff behind it.
to be more exact,
many's a dogowner

throws the dog they've tired of
down onto the rocks.

It happens mainly at night.
The dogs die with a thud.
The tide washes the bodies away.

Nando told us too
how in the Spanish Civil War
not just dogs
but people –
maybe I caught him wrong but

after all, the wind from the sea
was blowing, loud and cold

DOG AND MASTER

Roco belonged
to this slaughterhouse worker
from somewhere near Madiswil.

Fat and happy
from eating so much meat,
shortlegged and above all
short of breath, the two of them were.

1977, I think it was.
The dog, at the wheels of a lorry.
The man, of a stroke.

(Translated by Donal McLaughlin
from Pedro Lenz, *Die Welt ist ein Taschentuch*
(Bern: Verlag X-Time, 2002))

Donal McLaughlin

The Swiss Way is Donal McLaughlin's provisional title for a work in progress inspired by a long-distance walk – the 'Weg der Schweiz' – inaugurated in 1991 as part of the 700th anniversary celebrations for the founding of the Swiss Confederation. McLauglin's account of walking this symbolic trail is designed to include passages, where relevant, on history, literature, art, and international football. (The walk was completed just minutes before the Swiss took on Croatia in one of the first fixtures of Euro 2004 in Portugal). The extract offered here forms the opening pages of the book.

Weg der Schweiz
A scenic trail
through William Tell country

Inaugurated in 1991 as part of the 700th anniversary celebrations of the founding of the Swiss Confederation, this trail leads you round the southernmost part of Lake Lucerne. The 35km route has 26 sections, corresponding to the 26 cantons in the Confederation, with each allotted a length of the path proportionate to its population. Every 5mm of the trail represents a Swiss citizen.

The trail begins on the Rütli Meadow, the so-called 'cradle of Switzerland', where the Confederation was founded in 1291, and takes you – via Seelisberg, Bauen, Flüelen, Sisikon & Morschach – to Brunnen.

A superb network of ferry, bus and train connections between different places along the way means shorter walks are also possible. Unbeatable excursions are guaranteed – for young and old, alike.

Welcome to the Weg der Schweiz! To William Tell country!

Morgenrot would've been nice: some crack-
of-dawn sunshine; a reddish tinge behind the
wooded hills beyond the trees & rooftops

around my mate's new place; some colour
in the sky to entice us onto the balcony.
Instead, the neighbour opposite saw two
Scots step out into a dreich, wet grey, the
rucksacks on our backs & boots on our feet
declaring our intentions for the weekend.
June in Zürich, for once, looking like mid-
bloody-November in Scotland.
The 8-minute drive to the office; the tram
to the station; and that 08.09 to Brunnen's
looking feasible. My mate deals with the
tickets as I announce a raid on the lower-
level bookshop. I know exactly where the
book is: the far back corner; under 'F'. The
receipt records the purchase at six minutes
past eight on a Saturday morning of a serious
work of literature.
We meet where we parted & head for Platform 6. Preparing to board, my mate spots
a problem with the ticket. It's a day return.
Doesn't permit you to overnight. He checks
with an official on the platform – to be told
to ask on the train.

The train moves off. I remove the book
from the bag – Säckli? the guy asked – for
an initial, cursory, glance. The blurb on the
cover, I'll discover, is the opening passage
of the book. It grabs me immediately: the
thought of a knight with no sense of landscape riding through the region we are about
to walk; thought of the Föhn wind making
the mountains seem closer than necessary;
of a plump knight praising the blossoming

cherry trees in order to be polite.
Es war heiß und blau.
A sentence like that should've dismissed any
notion of blurb.
It was hot and blue.
If only!
It was grey.
A grey just short of downpour.
And there's us: preparing to walk. To walk 5
millimetres per head of population.
'Seven million,' my mate informs me.
'A population of seven million, Switzerland
has – '
Fifth-of-an-inch citizenship, I later get
round to thinking.
Immerhin.

Our tickets are checked & the guy confirms
our suspicion: they won't be valid tomorrow.
'What can we do?' we ask.
'Ask in Brunnen' is as much as we get as the
buck's passed onto the next guy.

Soon, we're discussing service. My tour of
the second-hand bookshops: Sagt Ihnen der
Name César Manrique was? Or: Ist Ihnen
der Künstler César Manrique ein Begriff?
And every time, just: Nein. Not: let me
look it up and see. Not: let me just check
the computer to see. But: Nein. A Nein that
allows nothing but Also, auf Wiedersehen,
in dem Fall.

The one exception: the man who stepped
out of his shop to point me up & along &
up again to Zähringer. But even he was nur
ein bißchen offen: actually, he was closed
for stock-taking.

My mate agrees: 'They just don't care!'

He tells me the tale of the CD player for
his new flat. How he was asked to return
another day as the assistant, currently alone,
would have had to go to the storeroom. How
he caught another branch, in Schlieren,
minutes before it closed. How he heard one
colleague tutting as the other agreed to serve
him. How the one who did was brand-new
as he re-packed the display model.

I catch a woman, listening, just as she's
caught me, looking. Realise we're chatting
in English, but with serious German quotations. Look like backpackers we might,
ahnungslos we're not, though. We've got
the lingo to substantiate complaints. Idiom,
syntax, the works.

Your woman writes as we speak, filling page
after DIN A4 page. Our accents have been
noted, for sure. McCall Smith appears on
the table before her. Tears of the Giraffe.
Unopened.

'The latest Scot to take the world by storm!'
I tell my mate & nod.

I want her to know we've clocked her.

By ZUG, we're repacking our rucksacks: the
contents first placed in heavy-duty poly bags
I thought to lift as we left.

'It's gettin wetter, mate!'
'Fuck!'

Your woman catches me looking again: those
full red lips; her feet bare, and only just in
her sandals. The pen that never stops.
Italiana.
The announcements on the train are also
given in Italian.

The weather had brightened after ZUG, but
as we approach ARTH-GOLDAU, it turns
to filthy; the hillside opposite's barely visible;
the cloud-level halfway down the hill.
Hodler's Manövriermasse comes back to
mind; the explanations alongside paintings
in the exhibition in Zürich. The mountains:
fixed, givens, immutable topographical facts;
the clouds or mist more indeterminate,
surfaces he could manoeuvre, manipulate,
to achieve the desired effect.
I imagine disembarking briefly; seizing &
jettisoning cloud; staging the conditions
we'd hoped for.

SCHWYZ.
The greens of the slopes & trees finally
visible.
The poster for the Hodler exhibition comes
back to mind: Die Jungfrau von der Isenfluh
aus. The upper triangle of the Jungfrau; the
lower, of the valley below. The greens of trees
and grass I see before me now; the lines in
the landscape; the patterns.

The smallness of the painting on the wall after the gi-normous posters around town.

More light – but banks of cloud lie low, still halfway down the hillside.

The one person out in a boat has a brolly up.

Harry Potter 3: the only film in town, I see from the freebie newspaper.

BRUNNEN
Rucksacks on our backs, we disembark. On the platform, a tall skinny man has a bright white cello-case on his. The loopy side-view turns to rear-view & we follow the cello down into the subway.
The train-ticket confusion continues: nowt poss before tomorrow. Try in Flüelen in the morning, they advise; or return to Brunnen by six. We look at each other, confused. Back home, the day after would be way too late for changes.
It's a ten-minute walk to the boat, the book says. I'm aware we now have less.
The Ben Sherman jacket I should exchange for my waterproof absorbs first heavy rain-drops.

Shades of Grey.
The title of the Marzaroli book on Glasgow sums up the view awaiting us. There's no depth to the image from the jetty: the

diagonals of dark mountainsides cutting
in from the left and right; the greys of the
sky & rain ensuring crap visibility; the
lake reflecting nothing – which, in itself, is
something.
I'm here; here to do this; but part of me's
now reluctant; could almost call it off.
A white boat pulls in from the right; to ferry
us off into two dimensions.
'It's all women doin this, mate!' I note as
we wait.

A quick coffee.
We pick up a leaflet sporting the image currently in triplicate on billboards: what looks
like a huge pencil's suspended over a boulder;
this, Magritte-style, before a background of
mountains & a lake.
the pits in the surface of the boulder –
Maybe it is Magritte?
Schiller's Wilhelm Tell, I know from another
flyer, will be performed on the Rütli this
summer. An open-air production, here from
Weimar, for the bicentenary.
The leaflet opens out; contains a montage of
images & words. SCHILLER asking Cotta
for gen on Swiss settings; daring to write
what he did though he'd never set eyes on
the Alps; his study plastered throughout
with every available map. GOETHE stressing how his colleague read every travelogue
going; acquainted himself with the history;
then sat himself down & didn't get up till
he'd finished his version of Tell.

MARK TWAIN saying he'd cross oceans &
continents to see the Rütli Meadow, off-the-
beaten-track & small, though it be.
TURNER's Bay of Uri.
HODLER's sketch for a painting of the
Rütli Oath.

On the boat, too, we glance at papers,
leaflets.
My mate points out how the route first
climbs, sets off in the 'wrong' direction, then
turns & back-tracks to work its way down
to, and round, the lake. The Urnersee. Our
part of the Vierwaldstättersee. The Lake of
the Four Forest Cantons, known, in English,
as Lake Lucerne.
Typical me: doing my homework only once
I get there.

One map has the two-character codes of
the twenty-six cantons entered along the
route.

I nip to the loo. Return to see I'm missing
something: a rock with an inscription.
'Yeah, there's a Schiller Rock,' my mate recalls, 'visible only from the boat.'
I've missed it. Must hope the Internet or a
book can supply the details.

We disembark. Unpack the waterproofs &
pull them on.
Our route's to be marked by marble stones,
representing the cantons.

My mate confirms my suspicion: the sequence reflects the order in which the cantons joined.

*   *   *

We set off.
The women seem to stand back, expecting us men to plough on; I – typically – hesitate, give them the option to lead.
They don't.
A shared glance, and my mate & I go for it; dig in to set a pace, to get some distance between us.

Our first walk in yonks. Almost immediately, I'm gasping. The gradient, unrelenting, catches me out. My breathing's noisy; resists attempts to regulate it.
I focus on the kagoul ahead of me.

rain forest water sky

rain forest water sky

rain forest water sky

Thou shalt not fall behind.

Still, the desire not to breathe so noisily; to get the breathing regulated.

the path climbs. the clouds hang. the trees drip. the rain falls.

the path climbs. the clouds hang. the trees
drip. the rain falls.
the path climbs. the clouds hang. the trees
drip –

The cowbells I hear are on sheep.

Up ahead: two women with brollies – one
pink, one blue – who weren't on our boat.
Pinkbrolly's in blue trousers & Bluebrolly's
in pink. Colour coordination which seems
to spell sisterhood.
We overtake them.

My mate stops, unexpectedly.
URI 1291
I read on a stone, with the Swiss Cross
symbol for our walk.
'These are what we have to look out for – '
I think back to thistles, carved on wooden
posts, on the West Highland Way in Scot-
land.
The second stone soon follows:
URI 1291   SCHWYZ 1291
I read, now anticipating a history lesson.

Soon after that, we're looking up into the
trees; breaking our necks to cope with the
gradient. Three sections of a huge waterfall
are visible; the water crashing down.
We continue, blinkered by plastic hoods.
'Don't know about you, but I'm as wet on
the inside as the outside already!' my mate

comments, just as I anticipate a shower that
evening.

OBWALDEN 1291
and
NIDWALDEN 1291
follow. Cantons with small populations.
Forest cantons, as I'll read, days later.
We're not out of the trees yet.

Stones for cantons –
and cheap plaques that give God the credit
for all the beauty surrounding us.

the clouds hang. the rain stays.
the path climbs. the water falls.
the trees drip. a dog barks.
the mud gives.

puddles gather.

beyond us blurs.

(Extract from Donal McLaughlin,
*The Swiss Way. On walking the
'Path of Switzerland'* [a work in progress])

Interviews with Writers

Joy Charnley

Portrait of a Poet:
an interview with Marie-José Piguet

Marie-José Piguet was born in the *Pays de Vaud* in 1941. In 1972 she married the painter Lionel Knight and moved to Cornwall and then Exeter in Devon, where she still lives. In 1974 she won the *Prix Georges Nicole* for her first novel and has gone on to publish another two novels and a collection of short stories. She returns regularly to Switzerland, particularly her native canton. She comfortably inhabits both the French and English languages, a fact which was rather neatly illustrated when some of the responses in the following interview came spontaneously in French and others in English.

> *Reviens, ma douce* (Vevey: Galland, 1974; Lausanne: L'Aire, 1989). Prix Georges Nicole 1974; Prix Alpes-Jura 1975.
> *Jean Fantoche. Portrait bouffon d'une auguste famille* (Vevey: Galland, 1981). Prix Schiller   1981.
> *Une Demoiselle éblouissante* (Lausanne: L'Aire, 1987).
> *Petits contes d'outre-Manche* (Lausanne: L'Aire, 1990).

England/United Kingdom

JC   You write a great deal about characters who do not feel as though they are in the right place and who consequently move away, often going into a sort of exile (Reviens ma douce, Une Demoiselle éblouissante). *Does this reflect your own experience of moving to another country?*

M-JP I am sure it does. Unconsciously maybe, for I remember a dream that I had probably around my departure for England in 1970 which I related in *Écriture* 37 (pp. 131–135). It was in answer to a questionnaire on the theme of exile. But I think it is deeper than that. I would go as far as to say that the exile some of my key characters are experiencing is explained by their unmet aspirations within the world they live in. Their deep-down identity (hidden, since the world around them does not recognise or accept it) is therefore at stake, hence their feeling of exile. The notion of *âme soeur* represents, if you like, the stake needed by the exiled character to feel more grounded in a hostile and alien world. This is illustrated by the character of Zélie in *Jean Fantoche*. In *Jean Fantoche*, after the death of her husband, Zélie is confronted with such an exile in the world now deserted by her *baladin*, her 'light', her 'guide' (p. 22), this world where she cannot find her place anymore and which she is thinking of leaving. Because life in this world is a passage and death its climax, this world cannot be whole. Cannot be home. However she will make a U-turn as spring is showing signs of new life, of hope, of 'une plus belle aurore' (p. 22). In *Une Demoiselle éblouissante* the malaise of the main character, Armande Lebeau, is quite different. There is no question of soul there but of ambition. Although Armande may feel she has at last found her place in the world, in the end the world is depriving her of what she thought she had acquired – renown, celebrity – simply because fashion has changed and has left her behind. The new generation has taken her place. Now, had she been 'with it' her position as a well-known *couturière* might have held for a time, but only for a time since everything is doomed to pass, be it work or a person. I have enlarged on the problem of exile in a slightly different manner in my as yet unpublished novel *Mademoiselle J. grimpe sur scène*, by threatening my main character, Astrance Juniper, with losing her identity through her inability to secure herself a rôle in the fabric of society. The world in this novel is a theatre stage where the bold, the strong and the favoured play their rôles while the rest of humankind is doomed to watch without being able to take part. This is one *volet* of what rootlessness and exile is about. The other *volet* being a more abstract, spiritual exile.

JC   *In* Une Demoiselle éblouissante *you describe England as 'cette terre mystérieuse à l'odeur d'algues et de sel posée à cheval sur la mer du Nord et l'Atlantique, engloutie dans le silence des brouillards, estompée par les brumes, pelée par les vents... Ce pays amoureux de traditions' (p. 129). What were your mental images of the country before you first visited it, what impressions did your first trip there leave and how would you now describe England and its inhabitants?*

M-JP   I did not imagine England beforehand. I was ready for impressions. And they certainly left their marks on me. It was in 1961. I came to Somerset as an *assistante de français* in an old-fashioned Grammar School for girls. The school consisted of four or five Victorian houses joined together by dark corridors all overlooking the Bristol Channel, the old pier and the town of Weston-super-Mare. Strong winds coming from Wales rattled the guillotine windows and swelled the black gowns of the teachers, adding an atmosphere of 'Wuthering Heights' to the scene. Dramatic, awe-ful and thrilling. The pupils in uniforms were all girls, rather mad and childish especially the older ones. Each had their little fetish on their desk: a bear, a frog, a sheep and in their midst, I was the oddity, the curiosity. The school traditions, like chapel before class, the long refectory tables at meal times, the dormitories, the smells, the sea, the landscape and my old-fashioned Victorian room, it all felt like living on another planet. It was a revelation to me. I was discovering a new life. England changed radically in the seventies while she tried to merge with the Continent. First decimalisation, the education system, the levelling of classes or at least the effort towards it, the endeavour to eradicate what made England different from the Continent. In spite of that England remains very much English and unlike the nucleus of Europe. What strikes me now is the lack of aesthetics and capacity for making something enjoyable out of the ordinary things of life. Like eating, for example, or dressing, the decor in general, taking one's time over things, all these little details that would make everyday life pleasurable. Instead, one has the feeling that basic things are basic things; they have to be done – quickly, effectively – and done with.

JC   *Again in* Une Demoiselle éblouissante *you have a rather nice turn of phrase to sum up the difference between the UK and Switzerland, declaring the former to be 'ce pays posé à côté de l'Europe aussi dissemblable de leur continent que l'est un melon d'un brugnon' (p. 130). Do you really feel that the UK is very different from the rest of Europe? Would it be true to say that the UK and Switzerland share a certain distrust of Europe or are the two countries in fact very different in this respect?*

M-JP The answer to this question is partly found in the former one. But, yes, I do think England is very different from, say, France or Italy and Spain. I believe that England shares a special friendship with Italy. Is it their difference in mentality that attracts them to each other like one says that 'les contraires s'attirent' (opposites attract)? As regards her relationship with Switzerland, I would say that the two countries share a common stubbornness which is rooted in their respective traditions. They have a loathing for change. Their pace is slower. Their people are more conservative and *réfléchis*. Less show-off than the Latin races. They are more objective, rational, and seem to lack fantasy, adventure and imagination. They share discretion yet not the same discretion. The English are discreet in regard to their emotions; the Swiss toward facts and deeds. Geographically, both England and Switzerland are surrounded by sea or mountains which may explain their common isolation. But these considerations should be taken as a few dabs of paint on a canvas. They are some of the views I have, indeed feelings, and therefore totally personal.

JC   In the short story 'L'Etrangère' in Petits Contes d'outre-Manche *the central character is told: 'l'étrangère, c'est vous' (p. 8). Have you felt or do you sometimes still feel foreign in the UK? How does this foreignness manifest itself? Do you ever feel out of place in Switzerland?*

M-JP Part of myself has remained a foreigner whether in England or in Switzerland. In England, I am a foreigner in the way I speak or express myself, in the way I behave, in the way I dress, in my manners, my vision or indeed my behaviour regarding eating, in my way of thinking or reasoning. In Switzerland, I feel a foreigner because of the distance – in time and experiences – that separates me from my country. After 30 years of absence, I have become more critical. Distance has revealed the flaws and shortcomings of the country of my birth (as of course of England too). It is an enlightening position to be in for seeing things in their true light. One could illustrate this by the image of the painter who needs to take some steps back in order to judge her or his work more realistically. But it is the position of an outsider. Of a foreigner.

JC   Is it easier to observe a country when one is an outsider/foreigner? Do you feel you have a privileged view of both countries?

M-JP Since this question is now answered, let me just tell you what one of my readers asked me about my *Petits contes d'outre-Manche*: 'What was your standpoint when you wrote these short stories? Which way were you looking?' My answer was: 'Both ways. Sometimes across the Channel to the Continent, sometimes with my back to it.'

JC   Have you written texts in English?

M-JP Yes, poetry in particular and short prose. I translated 'Courtship' (*Petits contes d'outre-Manche* p. 17) which I sent for the mini-saga competition launched by the *Daily Telegraph* and the Arvon

Foundation. It was published in their anthology in 1999. I have taken poetry workshops with an English poet called James Harpur and this has opened a new horizon for me as regards expressing myself in English. But I love the French language so much that I have not yet brought myself to write a long piece in English.

Landscapes

JC   Your three novels are very clearly set in Switzerland, for example Jean Fantoche *which evokes marvellously the* Vallée de Joux. *Is the Swiss landscape (mountains, lake), in particular the* Pays de Vaud, *important to you (in your writing or in a more general way) and do you miss it when you are in the UK?*

M-JP I started to write seriously after I left Switzerland. It's as if going away had triggered the desire in me to write. As if distance had heightened my awareness of what I had just left: family, child-hood, landscapes – in a sense, my roots – and had given all that a new sheen, a new light, made it appear to me anew. This is probably why in *Reviens, ma douce* (p. 102) Joëlle feels this urge to be 'le chantre de notre histoire' in order to save this 'univers minutieusement créé' from the passing of time, from oblivion. And it was precisely this creative act – 'writing' – that would give it a new life.

JC   You write more about familles paysannes *and rural environments than about cities. Do you find urban environments less inspiring?*

M-JP Quite simply because those were the families I knew best since I grew up with them. Townies, unlike country people, do not share the same intimacy with nature, that extra sense which both elevates and relativises human beings confronted with nature. This is a generality of course. Nature was my first source of inspiration, the place where I grew up surrounded by people who made me love it. Having said that I am interested in all human beings irrespective of their provenance. I am fascinated by the way people relate to one another, their idiosyncrasies, their characters, their behaviour in the face of love, family, work, careers, ambition, growing old, ill, facing death. What place, if any, they give to the 'sacred' in day-to-day living. Whether or not they consider life as a sacred affair.

JC   Human idiocy comes through in many of your stories. Do you generally feel that human beings have a globally negative impact on the world? Do you feel it is important to try to have a positive influence on the environment?

M-JP   I am surprised that the term 'idiocy' was what came to your mind when you read my texts. For idiocy is debilitating and it was not in my intention to convey such an idea. Rather I wanted to show humans' lack of vision and indeed intelligence, the stupidity and ridicule of such characters that are infatuated with their own importance, their position in society, their influence, the belief in their superiority over others. I wanted to make fun of these characters that have lost all humility and modesty, all lightness of being; such characters who do not realise that whatever they are or have is a gift that they are graced with. In *Une Demoiselle éblouissante* there are two types of characters: those who live in tune with nature, who consider life as sacred, and those whose ultimate goal is to succeed and dominate. That is why, at the beginning of the book, I quoted a phrase from G.K. Chesterton who, when asked why angels flew, replied something like: because they do not take themselves seriously.

Writing/creation

JC   Your writing is often reminiscent of Catherine Colomb (Châteaux en enfance, Les esprits de la terre, Le temps des anges)*, whose writing I know you are very familiar with. Monique Saint-Hélier* (Bois-Mort,

Le Cavalier de paille, Le Martin-pêcheur, L'Arrosoir rouge) *is also a writer who comes to mind. Can you say something about your thoughts on these writers, what appeals to you in their writing and how important an influence they were/are for you?*

M-JP It was after the publication of *Reviens, ma douce* that my publisher pointed out to me *un cousinage* between my writing and Catherine Colomb's. I had never read anything by her, in fact did not even know her. On reading her work I immediately recognised what I call a *littérature-du-dedans* as opposed to an external one. Rollo May in *The Courage to Create* (a book I have only just discovered) calls it respectively 'the mechanical form' (external to the poet) and the 'organic form' or 'inner form' where the passion of the poet is transmitted through her/his work. Monique Saint-Hélier is one of these *poète-romancières* who enchanted me. But it was Colette and Saint Exupéry, both of whom are 'organic' or 'inner-writers' and poets who gave me the desire to write. They stimulated me rather than influenced me. They imparted to me this driving force that was to set me writing about my world, my own world. The first title of *Reviens, ma douce* was *Dis-moi ton monde* – the question of a mother to her daughter. Bertil Galland did not like it and we eventually chose *Reviens, ma douce*. Another facet of the *cousinage* between Colomb's writing and mine is that they are both *écriture blessée*: death of the mother for Colomb, of the father in my case. Both Colomb and Virginia Woolf's *écriture-du-dedans et en cercle* confirmed me in my way of expressing myself – that is in an anachronic and recurrent form rather than what I call the *und nachher* (*et puis, et après*, 'and then next') form.

JC   *Do you have any thoughts on contemporary literature in Switzerland and the United Kingdom?*

M-JP As a general rule I don't read fiction because I think that all novels are the same. Apart from those which are different and there aren't many of them. Fiction, though I have and occasionally indulge in it, is not my preoccupation at this time of my life. There are more substantial readings that come first. However, for me literature is first and foremost an art. And art is an author's personal vision. To quote *The New Oxford Dictionary* on the meaning of vision: 'a person who or thing which is apparently perceived otherwise than by ordinary sight'. So I perceive art as being the author's vision of reality (his/hers or others) transposed, transcended, and where truth and craft (or call it style, virtuosity, skill) entwined will produce something arresting and astonishing. Astonishment ('étonnement', see *Le Robert*) is a surprise caused by something out of the ordinary, out of the expected. Poetry may be a better means of conveying art in literature. Allow me here to quote J-P. Monnier in an interview he gave to the *Passe-Muraille* in April 1992: 'La littérature d'aujourd'hui, en Suisse romande et ailleurs, me paraît plus objective. Elle est moins engagée subjectivement que celle que nous avons connue [...] Comme on ne se paie plus de mots, aujourd'hui, on ne croit plus tellement que la vraie vie est absente ou que nous ne sommes pas au monde – ce sont des mots de Rimbaud. Il n'y a plus cet engagement politique, au sens large, ou cet engagement métaphysique'. J. Chessex, in an article published in December 1995 in the same paper, spoke of poets (again in a wide sense, that is novelists included) of being 'métaphysiciens'. Today the race of these 'écrivains-métaphysiciens' is extinct or nearly so. Literature has to fit in with the expected, the marketable, the materials of our times if it wants to succeed. But it surprises no more. I don't read for the story but to enjoy the construction, the form of expression, the symbolism and the poetic imagination, the style and the message. In fact literature in *Suisse romande* corresponds (or used to correspond) to these criteria, which is not often the case in recent British or even French writing. I am not at all systematic in my reading and I tend to read whatever I feel like, a book recommended by people who have similar tastes to me for example. But these past few years my reading has been centred on my research on Colomb: theology, psychology and philosophy.

JC   Although your style is very different from that of writers such as Suzanne Deriex (Les sept vies de Louise Croisier née Moraz, Un Arbre de Vie, Exils, La Tourmente) *you appear to have a similar interest in families and the tradition of the 'family saga'. Would it be fair to say though that you are more interested in creating an atmosphere than telling a story?*

M-JP It could be so though all my novels have a story: the life story of my characters. Can I here make a difference between a 'plot' – the English equivalent for *intrigue* – and a 'story', *une histoire*. In that sense, yes, I am not a 'plot writer' but a *Sagen writer* if you allow me this German-English expression. I write about 'life'. Somewhere Virginia Woolf wrote this sentence of which I remember only the end: 'the truer the facts, the better the fiction'.

JC   You also seem to take a great interest in women and their lives. Would you describe yourself as a feminist and does the term écriture féminine *have any meaning for you?*

M-JP I would not describe myself as a 'feminist writer' in a political sense. Anyway politics are not my thing whether they are red, blue or whatever. But I am certainly interested in *women*. Women's psyche, emotions, reactions, views on life in general. Being a woman physically, psychologically, philosophically, spiritually and practically. That is what I would say is the material of *une écriture féminine* as against *une écriture féministe*.

JC   In several short stories in Petits contes d'outre-Manche *you discuss the theme of money and generosity or lack of it ('Le jeune homme riche', 'Propos d'un avare'). Being a writer or painter implies giving something of oneself, one's art, vision, imagination; what does an artist or writer expect or hope for in return? Have you personally been pleased or disappointed with any of the reactions to your writing?*

M-JP To be read, recognised (be it only by a small but perspicacious category of people); to touch the reader's sensitivity and intelligence; to open in the reader's mind a sense of the sacred (reflected, in this case, in one's literature) and to trigger in them the desire to express in their turn their own sensitivity in whatever forms; to stimulate the interest of scholars and researchers – some of these desires have been met with. But the sacred – or can we call it the more serious aspects, the spiritual issues, in the arts – seem today to be thin on the ground. The kind of literature I am talking about is disappearing. Fashion has moved on and commercial forms have taken over. This is what puzzles and saddens me.

JC   In 'Le Trésor' you talk about another kind of wealth, the hidden talents we all possess; you ask:'N'êtes-vous pas comme moi porteurs et porteuses de perles? Qu'attendez-vous donc pour vous mettre au travail?' (p. 57) and talk of 'deux petites femmes extraordinaires, deux originales qui se prenaient pour des huîtres' (p. 58). Do you believe that many people have talents, 'hidden pearls' (for example a talent for writing or painting) which they do not exploit, or are such creative activities much more rare than is commonly thought?

M-JP 'Le Trésor', which gives its name to my short story, is precisely the spiritual component of each human being, the breath of life which makes us aware, conscious of the spirit, the transcendental. On this subject read 'How the Bee Became' in Ted Hughes's *How the Whale Became and Other Stories*. Charisma itself is a talent but it is 'a divinely conferred power or talent' (Oxford Dictionary). It is a *gift* and that is why we should not boast about it. Rather we should be grateful for it and use it in a creative purpose (in whatever form) like these 'deux petites femmes extraordinaires, deux originales qui se prenaient pour des huîtres'. These two characters had recognised the presence in them of a pearl.

JC   Your writing is full of subtle humour and yet a darker side is never far away; does it seem inevitable to you that there should be this mix, or have you ever written (or attempted to write) completely comic pieces?

M-JP Wouldn't you say that some of my *Petits contes d'outre-Manche* were purely comic, that is without a trace of darkness in them? Like 'Noce' (p.10), 'Sa Majesté la tête en bas' (p. 21), 'La tête de mon bien-aimé' (p. 78), 'Encore une précieuse ridicule' (p. 36-37) though irony is never far away in this text. As, in fact, in quite a lot of *Petits contes d'outre-Manche*. But is irony necessarily dark? Otherwise, no, I have never tackled any solely comic subjects so far.

JC   What makes a writer exceptional or different from a non-writer?

M-JP I don't think writers are more exceptional or different from non-writers. Musicians, painters, sculptors or simply good cooks, brilliant entertainers, fabulous lovers or good gardeners may be just as exceptional. Writers express themselves in words while others do it in a multitude of other ways. What makes someone exceptional is their desire, capacity and will to create. Whatever the creation: lovemaking, food or a fabulous garden.

Mothers and daughters

JC   In several of your novels and short stories, the theme of relations between mothers and daughters recurs (Reviens, ma douce, Jean Fantoche, Une Demoiselle éblouissante). *Very often the mother encourages her daughter/s to study/leave home/achieve ambitions and yet at the same time she feels ambivalent about this since she misses her daughter/s and somewhat regrets having encouraged them to leave. In* Jean Fantoche, *for example, Zélie laments: 'Elles avaient grandi. Trop même. Comme elle [Zélie] aurait voulu pouvoir les en empêcher, les retenir de pousser, refaire de ses filles ses deux bébés joufflus' (p. 27) and in* Une Demoiselle éblouissante *Alberte exclaims: 'Quand je pense que j'ai tout fait pour qu'elle [her daughter] s'en aille, qu'elle voie du monde, qu'elle voyage! Si seulement elle [Alberte] pouvait se résoudre à le trancher une fois pour toutes ce cordon de chair qui la reliait à sa fille. Impossible' (p. 99). The daughters do not experience much difficulty with leaving, it is rather the mothers who suffer. Is this something you were aware of yourself as a daughter or is it a more general observation on families? Do you think it is inevitable that mothers should feel this ambivalence?*

M-JP Although I have never been a mother I can imagine the feeling of sudden solitude that mothers might feel when losing their daughter/s – or their son/s for that matter – when the moment comes. Whether the child has been the beneficiary of much sacrifice on the part of the mother or not. It is a *rite de passage* which is more painful for the party who is left behind – the mother as it happens – than for the child who has got life ahead of her/him. Of course there are mothers and mothers. Possessive ones and their counterparts. Mothers whose selfish pride to have a famous daughter may be stronger than the emotional tie (as seems to be the case with Margot and her daughters in the same novel). But on the whole I believe that family ties are stronger on the Continent than they are in England. That could be due to the fact that, traditionally, many English families used to send their children to boarding schools at an early age thus creating more independence from the start on both sides.

JC   Do you think mother/daughter tension is an inevitability or a myth?

M-JP It is certainly not an inevitability. Not every mother/daughter relationship is one of tension. It is a myth in the broader sense given to this term which is 'fiction', 'illusion' or even a 'lie'. But it is not a myth as myth should be understood: something 'essentially true'. In that sense tension between mothers and daughters can be essentially true though not inevitable.

JC   *In* Reviens, ma douce *your narrator speaks of taking 'tout l'essentiel pour un exil' (p. 113) and having in her suitcases, unbeknown to her mother, 'toutes les saisons' (p. 114). She also declares that 'j'emportais ma vie, ma foi, puisque je fuyais' (p. 114). For you was leaving Switzerland an escape, an exile, both or something else altogether?*

M-JP   Big question. Leaving Switzerland was neither an escape nor an exile, or at least not consciously. I simply followed my heart. And in turn the head followed the heart. It is with hindsight that I wrote about it in *Écriture* 37 (pp. 131–5) in a text called 'L'Etrangère' (the title of one of my short stories in *Petits contes d'outre-Manche*). The text was my answer to the question 'Votre "exil" joue-t-il un rôle dans votre création? Modifie-t-il votre regard sur la Suisse? Dans quel sens?'

Motherhood

JC   *Women who are mothers and others who choose not to be are central to much of your writing. In* Reviens, ma douce *you write: 'J'ai peur de n'avoir pas le coeur d'une mère' (p. 47) and your narrator has some fairly savage thoughts about the babies she is looking after at the hospital:*

> Quand je connaîtrai l'amour, ce ne sera pas pour enfanter. [...] Je n'aurai jamais de vie dans mon ventre et, pour me venger, j'avais envie d'étrangler ce petit corps chaud, moite d'énervement. Je pensais à le jeter dans la rue noire, à le laisser choir et qu'il s'enfonce, là, dans ma stérilité [...] C'est ridicule de parler de fils. Tu ne ressembles à rien. [...] Tu serais le fils de l'homme qui m'attend, là-bas, et m'écrit de revenir. Et puis non, tu es trop laid et tu ne fais que tourmenter ma nuit. (pp. 47–8)

Alice Rivaz thought that women who want to create need to choose between creation and writing and others (Corinna Bille, Anne-Lise

Grobéty) have written of the difficulty of combining both roles and of having almost to hide this activity from their family. Do you think that the situation has now changed or is being a writer always more difficult for a woman?

M-JP I don't really know since I have never had a family. But I would say – in the line of what I know – that writing, for women in general, is more difficult than for men since women are by nature expected to be 'au four et au moulin'. Though women are supposed to be good jugglers, able to do several things at the same time (while men are known to only concentrate on one thing at a time) it is precisely for that reason I believe that women have difficulty in concentrating on one thing at a time only. However for a woman like Jane Austen for example who must have been a woman of some leisure (no husband, no children; domestics to do the chores in the house), the 'having [...] to hide' her writing from her family is another issue altogether. In her days women were not expected to be 'public artists' hence her anonymous signature 'a lady' or the choice of male names behind which to hide for some women writers of the nineteenth century. The present situation is certainly easier since men – fathers – are now sharing in the task of family duties.

JC   The leitmotif of maternity recurs in several short stories ('Mater-nité' in Petits contes d'outre-Manche*); what does this signify for you?*

M-JP The 'Maternité' as described in the short story you mention, is another facet. In this precise case I am referring to a symbolic one: my character is pregnant with joy; with the seeds of happiness, of serenity; she has given birth to a new self, a spiritual being. In another short story, 'Félicité' (as yet unpublished) a woman is expecting but when the time of giving birth comes nothing happens. Maternity has turned into maturity. So who knows what meaning the word 'maternity' might hold for me in the years to come?

Politics

JC   You were born in the canton which was amongst the first to accord women the cantonal vote (in 1959, when you turned 18!) and you left Switzerland in the year when women gained the federal vote, 1971. Did these events seem important to you at the time?

M-JP   Not in the least. I was in another world.

JC   Is political commitment important?

M-JP   Not really. If at all.

Love

JC   In Reviens, ma douce *your narrator declares of her future husband Mortimer, 'sans lui, le monde est impossible' (p. 197) and in 'Renouveau' (Petits contes d'outre-Manche) you write, 'je n'ai pas d'époux, [...] je n'ai qu'un seul amour et celui-là revient toujours' (p. 74). Do you believe in the notion of finding a 'soulmate'?*

M-JP   Yes.

Death/time

JC   The theme of death is already present in Reviens, ma douce *and recurs in several short stories in* Petits contes d'outre-Manche *('Madame Bette', 'Le Cerf-volant', 'L'Elu', 'Renouveau'). How would you sum up your personal philosophy on death? Do you have any religious beliefs?*

M-JP   That is a big question. But, by the way, *Jean Fantoche* is also a novel about death. Death and Life. Perhaps the most important of all. It begins with a desire for death on the part of Zélie. It ends with the death of Jean Fantoche though the protagonist's death has occurred at the start. But it also ends with life as the final choice of Zélie. Life won her. And that final victory of life over death is what I mean in 'Renouveau' (*Petits contes d'outre-Manche*). I have a hope (whether religious or not is probably irrelevant) – but it is only a hope – that our life on earth – its unique and personal history – will live on though it has to come to an end on this earth. Our lives are two-dimensional but the two dimensions have not and will not find their final unity in the temporal world. Hence the profound desire to create (as a challenge to death, to annihilation). To create or to transpose. Or as the theologian Paul Tillich has it, to 'consecrate' – con-sacrer – (in his case through thanksgiving; but writing for me is a form of thanksgiving): 'To transfer something that belongs to the secular world into the sphere of the holy. It is not transformed [...] but it is elevated to represent the divine'. In the act of creating there is a longing to elevate. This is the reason why I chose to undertake research on the writings of Catherine Colomb in order to underline the element of the spiritual or the 'sacred' in her work.

*JC   In 'Le Sablier', 'Nouvel-An' and 'L'Horloger' it is the passing of time which interests you and in 'Assurez-vous toujours...toujours as-surez-vous!' (*Petits contes d'outre-Manche) *you take a sardonic look at people's attitudes to risk. Do you feel you have led the life you would have wanted? Do you have any regrets or are you someone for whom this word is meaningless? Do you feel you have lived a free life, taking risks and living without a safety net?*

M-JP I don't think that I ever planned a life for myself. I took what came though I might have chosen other ways had they been possible. Regrets? Not really (we cannot have everything and I am grateful for what has been and is my lot). Yes I have lived a reasonably free life though I have not consciously taken many risks as such. A safety net is not a solution. For one thing, it may not be placed at the right place in the right moment. Or the meshes could be too wide apart or the fabric could rot with time. Destiny is destiny whether we plan it or not. It does not always work the way we intend it to. So why bother. Anyway, life itself is a risk to which everyone is submitted. Until of course we decide to put an end to it.

Conclusion

JC   What are your current plans with regards to writing?

M-JP I have an unpublished novel *Mademoiselle J. grimpe sur scène* for which I received a grant from Pro Helvetia and which needs to find a publisher. I hope one day to write a novel the theme of which has occupied my head for some time. But so far I have not found the incentive to do so mainly because of the lack of a publisher interested in what I write. I am no longer content to write just to keep manuscripts in drawers. Some two years ago I attended a poetry workshop in Exeter and started to write in English – something I would like to pursue. But again there is this deep need to find a publisher who believes in one's work and who will find ways and means to broadcast it – that is to give it life. Writing that does not see daylight is bound to fade away.

JC   Is there a question which has not figured in this interview but which you would have liked to have been asked?

M-JP The question/s could be: What, in writing, is considered worthy of seeing daylight? Being published and broadcasted? Being studied in schools or universities? Must it absolutely be commercially aimed and 'with it', up-to-date? Are there themes in particular and ways of presenting these themes (by way of a novel, short stories or poetry) which are preferable nowadays in the twenty-first century to what they were say twenty years ago?

(Exeter/Glasgow, November 2004 – June 2005)

* * *

Work in Progress

'Quand je vis je ne me sens pas vivre. Mais quand je joue, c'est là que je me sens exister.' (Artaud, *Le théâtre et son double*)

L'été remontait sur scène, ardent et magnifique, et ramenait du même coup, sur la terrasse d'une guinguette au bord de l'eau, la silhouette vieillie et quasi démodée d'une demoiselle Juniper oscillant sur ses jambes usées. C'est que chaque été, aux premiers beaux jours, un rayon de soleil la remettait à flot, une main invisible la tirait de l'ombre où elle avait déjà trop longtemps somnolé et la reconduisait toujours vers cette même terrasse de cette même petite guinguette au bord de l'eau où le mobilier, comme dans un décor, avait retrouvé sa place attitrée. Alors, dans un geste de glaneuse, elle rassemblait dans ses mains l'ample paquet de ses jupes à godets et s'installait là, avec ses pensées, face au lac et aux Alpes.

Or cet après-midi-là, on la verra, comme tous les étés, s'avancer de sa démarche de crabe, repérer dans un coin de la terrasse un siège resté inoccupé, ramasser dans un geste qui lui est devenu propre les plis de ses jupes grises à pois blancs et les glisser discrètement sous ses cuisses, sourire au souvenir bien précis de cet insecte minuscule sauvé des balayures un jour d'hiver et qu'un rayon de soleil avait rendu à la vie (une patte qui se déplie, puis l'autre, encore une autre, et les élytres...) prononcer tout haut qu'il n'y avait somme toute que bien peu de différence entre le décor d'une guinguette qui se rouvre, top! à

l'heure précise des ruches et des taupinières et celui d'une cathédrale
à l'ouverture des matines quand un roulement d'orgue amène les
choristes ou celui d'un tambour les artistes d'un théâtre forain, hésiter,
poussée par le souffle, dans son dos, d'un dieu dingue, à se hisser elle
aussi sur les planches comme si c'était là, sur scène seulement, qu'on
pouvait se permettre de dénouer son fichu, de retirer ses mitaines et,
comme l'insecte revenu à la vie s'élance à la verticale vers la lumière,
de jeter en l'air dans un geste de victoire son lourd chapeau cloche et
se mettre à chanter ou donner la réplique?

C'est que le monde se relevait lui aussi de toute la souplesse vi-
brante du printemps et rassemblait, dans un mouvement de fièvre
commune, la troupe des baigneurs sur les dalles tièdes de la terrasse.
Sous un ciel d'une exquise transparence, délicatement tendu d'un
bout du lac à l'autre et ramené à d'humaines dimensions par le feuillage d'un tilleul argenté, le lourd rideau rouge qui clôt la saison ou
l'annonce, se levait sur le décor d'un lac indolent et mou qui berce,
dans un geste maternel, le corps aérien des montagnes.

Mais la réplique ...

'Ah non, ma fille, tu ne vas pas te lancer dans une carrière
théâtrale! Le théâtre, ce n'est pas la vie, c'est du thé-â-tre. Une farce!
De la comédie!...' La réplique se noua dans sa gorge comme elle
se rasseyait face à l'effectif du bistro où des sommelières bronzées
ouvraient d'un coup sec des parasols bariolés tandis que les baigneurs,
entrés impérieusement sur scène, comme sous la baguette d'un leader,
laissaient tomber un à un, dans un bruit de cloche sonore, leurs lourds
souliers de fer.

C'est donc bien en spectatrice qu'elle resserra sous ses cuisses
l'ample pli de ses jupes à godets. [...]

Et elle était partie dans sa longue robe de laine en tricot où des
papillons de feutre, à jamais pris dans la griffe d'un point de croix,
s'étaient faits à l'idée de rester sur sa robe, partie les cheveux coiffés
d'un noeud fraîchement amidonné, autoritaire et glorieux sur sa tête,
mais qui n'avait pas, pensait-elle, le pouvoir aspirant de l'hélice ou la
puissance d'une paire d'ailes pour la soulever. Du moins c'est ce qu'elle

croyait, lourde et mal à l'aise dans sa robe de laine, tandis que le sol se dérobait bel et bien sous ses pieds, que l'hôtel se rapetissait sous elle avec son jeu de quilles et ses sapins, que les têtes de ses camarades se renversaient sous le ciel:

'Mais où vas-tu Juni? Le bon Dieu n'habite plus là-haut, il n'habite nulle part le bon Dieu. Il n'existe pas. Redescends, on a des gaufres pour le thé et du sirop de grenadine!'

Comme ces petites guêpes sveltes qui planaient, immobiles, des minutes entières sur ses tartines de confiture avant de s'y poser, elle amorça la descente et faillit buter sur une quille à l'atterrissage. La bande aussitôt l'encercla. Toutes en jupettes courtes, cuisses nues et cheveux lâchés; elles promenaient leurs poupons en caoutchouc, tout nus déjà, alors que sa poupée – un vieux modèle en porcelaine – cachait sous ses robes et ses jupons les articulations ridicules de son anatomie.

'Tu l'habilles encore en hiver, idiote?'

Il faut dire que sans ses bas et ses culottes longues Marion aurait été la risée de la troupe et ça, elle ne l'admettrait pas. Et puis, elle n'avait pas comme les autres poupées ce petit trou entre les cuisses d'où pouvait sortir l'eau sucrée des biberons. Les langes des bébés-mouilleurs tombaient dans l'herbette; les frais, pliés en triangle, étaient fermement épinglés entre les cuisses dodues.

'Ote-lui son chapeau, bécasse! Retire ses bas et ses brassières! Montre-nous ses nichons, son derrière!'

'Elle n'en a pas!' déclara Emma.

'Fais voir!' hurla le choeur.

[...]

Sous les arbres d'un noir funèbre – qui n'étaient pourtant que d'innocents sapins – sa poupée, le chapeau de travers et les bas en tire-bouchon sur ses chevilles, posait, hanches coudes et genoux tordus, à poil sur une table du bistro.

Les bras en l'air, elle écarquillait ses grands yeux de verre sur un monde implacable tandis que dans le ciel d'un bleu scolaire on avait remonté les échelles, bouclé les battants… on verrouillait les portes et on la laissait seule dans le parc de l'hôtel communal.

Comment faire alors pour reprendre sa place au milieu de ces têtes narquoises qui l'épiaient de l'autre côté du mur et qui avaient pris soin de relever la passerelle derrière elles, celles de Rose et de Ferblantine, d'Odette et de la grande Emma, toutes ces têtes rouges, si rouges, alors que la sienne demeurait obstinément blanche?

Quelle force, quelle autorité, quelle main – non plus dans son dos cette fois-ci mais devant elle – allait enfin se tendre pour la reconduire au milieu du monde – ou de la terrasse, c'était pareil – et la convaincre de se joindre, dans un élan de fièvre commune, au déshabillage des baigneurs? de laisser tomber, comme eux et en même temps qu'eux, ses lourds souliers de fer?

[…]

Les bulles de l'été avaient beau monter, pétillantes dans les verres, et la presser de se mettre à l'aise, d'envoyer promener son attirail vestimentaire, la mécanique à laquelle elle avait toujours obéi la fit ramener sous ses robes le bout de ses trotters (comme autrefois ses sandales vernies de petite-fille, ses chaussures de montagne ou le mocassin rouge sous les bancs scolaires) tout comme elle ramenait sous leurs robes pourpres les souliers à boucles des enfants de choeur prêts pour la cérémonie.

Car qu'était-ce, sinon un spectacle, ce rassemblement de baigneurs sur la terrasse d'une guinguette et son décor en toile de fond: le lac où se miraient, vaines mais solides, les montagnes de l'autre rive?

Qu'était-ce sinon l'ouverture d'une heure de louange, d'un instant de prière dans l'extase joyeuse de l'été revenu: la terre et le ciel jumelés, les créatures et le créateur, les tables et les stalles, les baigneurs et les choristes, les serveuses et les bedeaux, les voûtes et le feuillage, le murmure des vagues et les antiennes du choeur…?

Tantôt l'éventail des voûtes reprenait ses droits et le cortège des enfants de choeur, collerettes empesées et mains jointes, prenaient la place des baigneurs pour entonner le Te Deum ou le Jubilate, tantôt les voûtes s'ouvraient dans un geste d'invitation à la fuite et le choeur immense de l'univers prenait la relève. Holy! bourdonnaient les abeilles sur le chemin mystérieux tracé pour elles un premier jour du monde. Holy! s'esclaffaient les mouettes suspendues au souffle descendu des montagnes et elles se posaient sur l'eau avec la légèreté de pétales. Holy! murmurait-elle tout bas de crainte de se faire remarquer alors qu'elle aurait voulu le hurler, arracher son corsage, retirer ses bas, laisser tomber ses jupes et se jeter à l'eau la première avec ses taches et ses défauts.

'Mais voyons, ma Cocote, les Juniper, tu le sais comme nous, n'ont jamais aimé l'eau!'

Lo-lo-lo.... jamais-aimé-LO!

Est-ce que ces têtes d'acteurs – qui n'étaient finalement que des têtes de baigneurs ou était-ce le contraire? – est-ce que toutes ces têtes qui pourraient tout aussi bien que la sienne n'être que des têtes de spectateurs allaient l'intimider, arrêter net son élan un jour d'in-contestable printemps?

C'est ainsi que par ce bel après-midi d'été ardent et magnifique, une première victime, mal équilibrée sur ses pieds menus – était-ce un gamin des baigneurs sorti du tas de sable ou un enfant de choeur échappé du cortège qui s'élançait, sans savoir bien où ni comment... vers les stalles? à la dérive? – avait culbuté sur les dalles entre les tables des baigneurs endormis.

Mais oui, avance, c'est tout droit, tout plat, y a pas de marche; il suffit de te lancer si tu veux voir le monde!

Son encombrante culotte de caoutchouc le poussait... hop-hop-hop-voir-le-monde, en avant! Une espèce de holy! informulé mais déjà senti, un cri, une louange, envahissait sa grosse tête ronde qui frôla l'angle d'une table, l'évita de justesse.

Tu vois, c'est facile, il suffit de ...
et finit par buter contre la table voisine qui n'était là que pour jouer son rôle d'obstacle – gloire, on le sait, de toutes les courses.

Personne ne le remarquerait donc jamais ce malin génie dans son habit transparent, tendre ses pièges et guetter, le sourire aux lèvres, le cri pour lui triomphant de celui qui perd pied?

Mais déjà l'enfant se redressait dans son bagage de langes. Le derrière en l'air, il relevait sa grosse tête vierge et sereine et reprenait possession du monde.

(Extract from an unpublished manuscript:
Marie-José Piguet, *Mlle J. grimpe sur scène*)

Kate Griffiths and Laura Rorato

Voicing Difference:
an Interview with Silvia Ricci Lempen

KG/LR   You are an Italian national who moved to Switzerland and begun writing in French. How do you view your position as a writer? Does the issue of national identity interest you? Do you consider yourself a Swiss writer?

SRL   The first thing I should point out is that I did not start writing in French when I moved to Switzerland. I belong to two cultures. I went to a French school so I did not change language when I arrived in Switzerland. As for the question on national identity, I would say that I oscillate between three national identities: I feel Italian, I feel Swiss but also French, because my cultural background is French. Having three identities gives me a certain distance from the very concept of national identity and enables me to see something positive in it. I think that it is much easier for me to see aspects of myself in each of these three identities than it would be if I had a single identity and had to recognise myself entirely in it, as this identity would inevitably become a form of oppression. I therefore understand those writers who, having a single identity, decide to reject it, sometimes violently, as in the case of Elfriede Jelinek who developed a sort of hatred towards her Austrian identity. The comparison with Elfriede Jelinek stops there, of course. All I wanted to say is that in my case, having three identities enables me to get what is most interesting out of each of them and accept as inevitable the fact that every person is rooted somewhere. Finally, coming to the question of whether I consider myself a Swiss writer, I would say that, yes, I do consider myself a Swiss writer, but not because of the way I write or the themes I deal with. It is in any case extremely difficult to define *Suisse romande* literature in these terms, even though many attempts have been made. For instance, it is often said that *Suisse romande* literature is far less political than Swiss literature in German and is mainly characterised by an interest in interiority. I am not interested in this kind of approach as I think that it is extremely difficult to talk of national identity in terms of a writing style. However, from a sociological point of view, I feel I am a Swiss writer.

KG/LR Did being a foreigner affect your career in any way, or did it make you more open to issues of 'otherness'? Your literary works contain various autobiographical elements: do you agree with Anderson's definition of autobiography as 'a space of difference within discourse'?[1]

SRL   If I may, I would like to point out that I strongly dislike the term 'career' as I have never seen my work in terms of a career. Apart from the aforementioned issues concerning my national identity, intellectually I also have a multiplicity of identities, which manifest themselves in the variety of approaches and 'diversions' that led me to writing. I studied philosophy – I wrote my doctoral thesis in philosophy – and I became politically active within Feminism. From the age of eight I knew that creative writing would be my future, and this is very important in my identity as a writer, but before devoting myself to it I had to do something else. As for the second part of your question, concerning Anderson's definition of autobiography, I wonder whether, in my case, one could say that the opposite is true. Anderson talks of 'the space of difference

1   It is in these terms that Anderson summarises Barthes' approach to auto-
     biography, Linda Anderson, *Autobiography*, (London/New York: Routledge,
     2001), p. 72.

within discourse' whilst I would say 'the space of discourse within difference'. I would also like to distinguish two aspects within autobiography. The first book I wrote was about my father. It was entirely autobiographical and I do not hide this aspect: on the contrary, I declare it clearly from the start. In my later novels, however, as in many novels, there are various autobiographical elements but they are transformed. When talking about this first autobiographical book I feel like turning Anderson's definition upside down. Whilst writing it, I had the clear feeling that my task was that of re-inventing, re-imagining, therefore putting the discourse of imagination into my difference, which for me was a fact. So I was very happy when this book was awarded a prestigious literary prize in this part of Switzerland and the president of the jury declared that I had succeeded in transforming autobiography into literary discourse, and that what I had written was very far removed from 'testimony'. I am extremely pleased with this judgement as currently, in my opinion, the panorama of what we call literature is stifled by personal accounts: how I recovered from cancer, how I was abandoned by my wife, or how I coped with a disabled child and so on. On a personal level, I have a great deal of respect and sympathy for these stories, but they are testimonies. Literature is something else. By embarking on a totally autobiographical work, of course, I also ran the risk of producing a testimony. So having been told that I had avoided this was for me a source of great satisfaction. There is a chapter in my book where I talk about our family trips on Sundays and I ask myself why I am telling that story, fully aware in writing that passage that if one is unable to transport memories into the literary sphere there is no point in recounting them.

KG/LR In your books you often mention the importance of 'distance' in order to comprehend things and events. Was the choice to write in French a way of distancing yourself from the subject matter of your novels, or was it dictated by the need to appeal to a wider audience? I am thinking particularly of Un Homme tragique, *which* is *set in Italy and describes your childhood and adolescence in Rome.*[2]

SRL   Undoubtedly, the need to distance myself played a vital role in my decision to write in French. To be perfectly honest, however, I am not sure whether I would have been linguistically able to write this book in Italian because I had been writing and working through the medium of French for several years. Writing in Italian would have implied refamiliarising myself with my native language in a different way. I would have had to convert my mother tongue into a literary language, which at this stage of my literary development is a constant temptation but would have been hard then. At that time, French imposed itself as the language I mastered best but the issue of distance is extremely important too. I would add that, apart from the language, some of the stylistic devices I employed were also the result of this need to distance myself from the autobiographical subject matter in order to turn it into literature. However, dialogues were a problem I had to face, as those dialogues had taken place in Italian, and not simply in standard Italian but in an Italian with a strong regional accent, which was the way my father spoke. As a consequence, I tried to limit the number of dialogues. Where a dialogue was absolutely necessary, I tried to find some equivalent in French, rather than translating literally what had been said in Italian with a Rome accent. As for the issue of the audience, in fact, the opposite is true. If I had written the book in Italian and published it in Italy, the number of readers would have been larger as the Italian market is bigger than the Swiss one.

KG/LR I was perhaps thinking of the French market. Are your books read in France?

---

2   In the course of the interview frequent reference is made to the following books by Silvia Ricci Lempen: *Un Homme Tragique* (Lausanne: Éditions de l'Aire, 1991); *Le Sentier des Éléphants* (Lausanne: Éditions de l'Aire, 1996); *Avant* (Lausanne: Éditions de l'Aire, 2000).

SRL This, of course, is a different problem that concerns publishers in *Suisse romande* as a whole, not just mine. They are unable to penetrate the French market, they do not manage to get their books reviewed in French papers because the French are very chauvinistic and the competition is already very strong within the domestic market. As usual, everything works through 'clans' and if you have no contacts you are excluded. The situation is slightly different for Swiss German writers. Even though many of them also feel marginalised, they are far less isolated than we are because the Germans are much more ready to accept Swiss writers who write in German as part of their family. The French, instead, consider writers from *Suisse romande* as foreign writers, although we are not sufficiently exotic to be interesting as we write in French. Naturally, there are also some historical reasons behind this difference. After the War, German-speaking Swiss writers were able to say things that German writers couldn't say because they were on the side of the losers. This created links between the writers of these two nations allowing the level of integration to be much higher today.

KG/LR Un Homme tragique *is currently being translated into Italian. How do you feel about it, given that Italian is one of your native languages? Are you playing an active role in this translation or do you allow the translator complete freedom?*

SRL My translator is excellent particularly when dealing with dialogues, which for me, as I have previously mentioned, were problematic from the start. She is perfectly bilingual and she seems to have the ability to recapture what had actually been said in Italian. When dealing with more descriptive passages we encounter a few more problems, partially because my style is rather complex, but also because of the nature of Italian as a language. French is much more fluid. A perfect example is the verb *to break*: *spezzare* in Italian, with the double z in the middle, is extremely harsh, whilst *briser* in French is much more fluid. When talking of Italian, I often use the metaphor of a sculpture made out of crystal, whilst the equivalent metaphor for French would be a sculpture made out of clay: as a consequence, a complex sentence in French inevitably flows better than in Italian, even if the translation is excellent. As for my role in the translation, when my translator sends me passages, I read them and make a few suggestions but I think that she should have the freedom to decide whether she wants to accept them or reject them. A translation is a new work and stylistic unity is very important.

KG/LR Have your works been translated into other languages?

SRL   No, just a few passages into English and Spanish at conferences. The translation of *Un Homme tragique* will be a first.

KG/LR You started your career as a journalist. Did you always know that you wanted to become a novelist? What kind of relationship do you see between these two forms of writing?

SRL   As previously mentioned, I have always been interested in creative writing. At the age of nine, when asked by my teacher at school to write an essay about what I wanted to do when I grew up, I wrote that I intended to become a writer. This was clear in my mind. What is less clear is why it took me so long to pursue my ambition, since I published my first literary work when I was forty. Personally, I think that this has something to do with my upbringing. I was brought up believing that duty takes precedence over pleasure. As creative writing for me represents the utmost pleasure, I had to postpone it until I had finished all the things I felt I had to do: writing a doctoral thesis, giving birth to two daughters and taking care of their upbringing. The other fundamental factor is that I knew that I could only approach creative writing by talking about my father, as my father was a person who had a huge influence on my life. He was both a terrible burden and an inspirational light, and I could not have dealt with these issues whilst he was alive. This explains why I took so many diversions in my life. However, your original question was about the relationship between journalism and creative writing. Well, I like writing all sorts of things, even a simple letter or an e-mail message: the physical act of writing gives me pleasure. As long as I can sit in front of a computer and write something I am happy. So journalism was the obvious job for me, it allowed me to combine my passion for writing with the possibility of earning a living. Initially, I drew a lot of pleasure and satisfaction from journalism. Later on, when I started devoting myself to creative writing, the two forms of writing started to compete with each other and the situation began to deteriorate: each year my suffering in having to set aside some time for my activities as a journalist became stronger and stronger. In the end I decided to give up journalism because, contrary to what most people believe, when one reaches a phase in life like mine, in which creative writing plays a fundamental role, journalism becomes an obstacle. In fact, I seem to remember that an English poet (possibly Ted Hughes, but I am not entirely sure), when asked why he had not tried to make a living by becoming a journalist, instead of working in a bank, replied that being a clerk was much more compatible with his literary vocation than going into journalism. Now I am teaching at university, which is also a very demanding job, but far enough from literature not to compete with it.

KG/LR You have always been interested in Feminism and for many years you edited the journal Femmes Suisses. *How do you view the issue of women's writing and gender studies? Do you see in these trends the risk of a new form of 'ghettoisation' or do you perceive them as genuine tools enabling women to have a voice of their own?*

SRL Let us say that I would like to make a distinction between the situation we had in the 1970s and the situation we have today. During the 1970s and 1980s women's access to writing was an extraordinary event and a fundamental element of the new, post-68

Feminism. The recognition that women had something different to say compared to what men had to say was very important. Women had to talk about their experience as women and express feelings that had been repressed for centuries. That was a very exciting and beautiful moment. Nowadays, the situation is rather different and I would be more reluctant to establish a link between women's writing and feminism. Personally, even though I read and enjoyed various books by feminist writers such as Monique Laederach (who, for instance, wrote a book entitled *La femme séparée* about a woman who decides to leave her husband to escape the stifling family atmosphere), when I entered the world of creative writing, I wanted to do something other than political activism. When I began writing my first book about my father, I was the editor of *Femmes Suisses* and I was dealing with feminist issues all the time. However, my interest in feminism was of a socio-political nature. By entering the world of creative writing, I wanted to experience something else. I consider myself both a feminist and a writer but not a feminist writer because I think that at this point in history, by which I mean the beginning of the new millennium and not the 1970s, women's literature as such does not carry the same revolutionary potential as it did then and can no longer be considered the artistic voice of feminist activism. This, of course, does not mean that literature should be totally devoid of a political message but simply that a piece of literature should not become a tool for political propaganda. My being a feminist and a writer are not totally different things, because I am the same person, but no one activity serves the other.

KG/LR References to history and current affairs are frequent in your books, particularly in Un Homme tragique *and* Le Sentier des Éléphants. *How do you view the relationship between* micro *and* macro *history?*

SRL   I am very pleased to hear that this aspect was noticed because my literary ambition is to reconstruct the totality of an individual, of my characters. In our experience as human beings micro and macro history are inexorably connected. Even when we are having a relaxed chat with friends in the garden over a glass of wine, macro history is present through the radio or other media informing us of events like the London bombings or the war in Iraq, and these facts stay in our hearts even when we are thinking about something else. In our unconscious, elements of micro and macro history have a symbiotic relationship and reciprocally influence each other. The perception of our personal circumstances is determined by bigger events around us and vice versa. As a writer, therefore, I am always striving to convey this continuum of feelings and sensations that can only be artificially kept apart. Even as a reader, what I like in a writer like Antonia Byatt, for instance, whom I greatly admire, is this symbiosis between the public and private spheres. Perhaps women writers – I am also thinking of two other writers whom I consider my role models, Margaret Atwood and Alice Munro – are more determined to make their readers perceive this unity in our experience of life. Male writers – although generalisations are always dangerous – can more easily separate the two spheres.

KG/LR   In Un Homme tragique *the physical deterioration of the narrator's father seems to be mirrored in the history of Italy, which is often referred to as a 'lost' or 'decomposing' country (HT pp. 65, 240). Likewise, Rome, with all its monuments and emblems of the past seems to acquire oppressive connotations and inspire a sense of guilt: 'Mais moi je ne veux pas, non, je ne veux pas porter sur mes épaules les malheurs de la terre' (HT p. 134); 'C'est tout près de chez nous. La via Ardeatina est une parallèle de la via Appia [...] on ne peut entrer là qu'à pas lents, comme pour se faire pardonner des morts l'obscénité d'être vivants' (HT p. 138). On various occasions the narrator appears to feel guilty for her lack of political engagement (HT p. 130). What is the role of a writer in society? Can art have a social function?*

SRL   It is interesting that you should point out the parallelism between the decline of the father and the Italian political situation because that was precisely the message I was given by my father throughout my childhood. He used to talk about Italy in terms of a country best forgotten. What is more, the physical decline of my father indeed took place during very difficult and tragic moments in Italian history such as the *anni di piombo*, the years of the Red Brigades. As for the sense of guilt, that is also true because guilt is part of everyday life. There is something fundamentally artificial when people pretend not to feel guilty or to be fully satisfied with what they do to improve the plight of humanity. Most individuals oscillate between moments when they are reasonably happy at having done something constructive (be it the simple act of joining an environmentally friendly organisation, or donating a small sum of money to a charitable cause) and others when they are fully aware that they do not do enough, or that what they do will not make a difference. What is certainly a feature of my characters is that they do not choose to be politically active. Personally, of course, I expressed my political engagement through Feminism. With my characters, instead, I wanted to stress this sense of doubt and un-easiness that inhabits each one of us. Finally, coming to the social function of art, as I mentioned previously, I do not like the idea of art as a tool for propaganda. If the only message of a work of art is a militant one or if the political message is too explicit, the artistic aspect of that piece of work suffers. What is very important instead, is for writers or artists in general – I am thinking of Umberto Eco or Salman Rushdie – to use the authority they have as successful artists to denounce cruelty and injustices throughout the world by writing to newspapers or through public speeches. This is something I also do from time to time. In this case, what we produce has nothing to do with art. If art can have a political message this must be achieved in a more subtle way. By appealing to the unconscious, the more elusive part of us, the part where our deepest thoughts and emotions are formed, where the factors that make us act in life develop, art can have an impact on our behaviour but not as a direct chain of cause and effect.

KG/LR Your works seem to be characterised by the recurrence of certain themes, the most striking of which is death. Even Le Sentier des Éléphants, *which is perhaps the most positive of all your books, opens with a reference to death. Why is the theme of death so central to your writing?*

SRL There is certainly something in me that is particularly sensitive to the idea of the death of a child as I think that this is the most horrible and traumatic experience an individual might have to face. I have friends who lost children and it is something I can only describe in terms of a deep sense of horror and despair, which is why it was important for me to deal with this in all my books. *Le Sentier* begins with the description of the death of a young boy, the protagonist of *Avant* has lost a child and even my latest book, the one I am currently writing, features a young person who comes very close to dying. As for death in general, it corresponds to one of my main literary and existential concerns, which is our human finiteness. This is perhaps more clearly visible in *Avant* but is present elsewhere too. In the autobiographical book, for instance, the figure of my father is an example of someone who cannot come to terms with necessity (the Greek goddess *Ananke*), and death, of course, is the most explicit example of necessity. Death is an extremely important theme for me precisely because it is the obvious manifestation of our finiteness. At the age of seventeen, when I was studying philosophy at school, I was given an assignment where I was asked to express my views on whether I thought that an individual should lead his/her life constantly thinking of the transience of all forms of life and experience, as suggested by Heidegger, or whether one should behave and act as if life were eternal, as suggested by Spinoza. Even then I already knew that what I was interested in was Heidegger's theory. From that moment onward I have always perceived death or finiteness as something constantly present in every single moment of my life.

KG/LR At the beginning of Avant, *Zen explains to David that, according to the Greek philosopher Zenon, 'le temps, et aussi l'espace, peuvent être divisés et redivisés à l'infini en unités de plus en plus petites, à l'intérieur desquelles Achille reste immobile. En somme, Zénon pretend que le mouvement n'existe pas' (A p. 9). How close is this notion to your own views on time and progress? The title* Avant *seems to contain this contradiction between two opposite moments (avant referring to the past but also implying a forward movement); yet many of your characters seem to feel, in a rather existentialist fashion, that there is no recuperable inner core of being that resists the ravages of time and change, and that the individual is in a permanent state of self-creation.*

SRL   This is a difficult question because it raises issues that are hard to express. I will try to answer by analysing the significance of the title *Avant*, a title that my publisher regrets having accepted because he thinks the book would have sold more copies if we had selected something less mysterious for it. For me, however, it was important to retain the original title for its symbolic value. I see in it two contradictory elements which are not so much those you mention but the idea of time and that of its possible non-existence. What I mean is that if there is an *avant* (a before), there is also a now and an after, proving the existence of time, but in *avant* I also see a reference to a situation, before Creation, where time did not exist. Before life emerged, and with it the notion of finiteness, everything was static. In my book there is a kind of nostalgia for that condition, a condition in which angst did not exist, as angst is caused by the flow of time (again, I am thinking of Heidegger). The reference to Zenon stresses this kind of nostalgia because, if movement does not exist, neither does time. I agree with the term 'existentialist' used in the question as angst is a key aspect of Existentialism.

*KG/LR Pascal's conceptualisation of man as 'un roseau pensant' and La Fontaine's fable of a reed bending but not breaking in the wind appear to occupy a prominent place in your work (*Avant *and* Le Sentier *in particular). Is it thought or the ability to bend that saves your characters?*

SRL   My characters usually differ from each other and in *Avant* I wanted to show different attitudes towards the issues raised in the question. For instance, David, the male protagonist, is someone who can bend and adapt to the curve of time. Mathilde, instead, is inflexible. Personally, I am convinced that only the ability to think and reflect, rather than a passive acceptance of life, can save the individual. Passivity is something alien to me but I felt it was important to explore this attitude through some of my characters.

KG/LR Characters' lives are peopled by the surfacing of earlier memories, likewise your texts are peopled by the periodic surfacing of earlier literary texts: certain texts are clearly cited and labelled; others are teasingly not attributed and the reader is left to pursue their thread, as Alissa in Le Sentier *pursues the thread of her research in the library. To what extent does your narrative play with notions of textual memory in relation to the reader and the narrative voice, as it depicts tales where notions of personal memories are explored?*

SRL   I have rather ambiguous feelings as regards the use I made of textual memory in my earlier books. In the current phase of my writing I am detaching myself from it. Perhaps I needed it initially because I was still too close to philosophy. My style was technically still rather discursive and I needed those references as a kind of support. I don't regret having done this but this aspect is almost absent in my latest novel. By keeping the bibliographical references to a minimum I wanted to avoid turning my novels into books of literary theory. In some cases, however, I wanted to give the reader the opportunity to explore the text I was referring to, if s/he wanted to. This phase has now been superseded and in the book I am currently writing I offer no help to the reader. The fact that even in earlier books I didn't always attribute all literary references indicates that I was striving to achieve the more independent style of writing I am experimenting with now.

KG/LR Whilst your work draws heavily on literature, the presence of the world of art is clear. The works of Delacroix, Mondrian and Munch are all used as filters through which characters describe their emotions. The language of your narrative likewise passes at times through the filter of art. It describes, for example, the landscape as a 'paysage préservé aux couleurs douces d'aquarelle' (Avant p. 196). Is this recourse to the image an attempt to show the insufficiency of the word, to underline that recourse to other media is necessary in order to communicate truly?

SRL   This is certainly true and I agree with Virginia Woolf when she says that, in a way, she regrets not being a painter and having to use words. When writing we are forced by the limitations of the medium to express things one after the other and the same applies to the reader whose experience of the work is also linear. When producing a painting instead, even though the physical act of painting implies a beginning and an end, this aspect is less important because the viewer has a global, synthetic impression of the work. Virginia Woolf explains very clearly the need for a writer to convey the totality of an emotion, of a specific moment in life, stressing that it is very difficult to do this with words. This is why in my books I often use brackets and very long sentences. It is my way of showing the complexity of each form of experience: whilst a character is experiencing something at the same time s/he might remember details from her/his past or start thinking about something else. This is also why I find pictorial or visual metaphors, which easily come to me, very useful. Like many writers of modernity I have this unsatisfiable longing for simultaneousness.

KG/LR The role of modern media in your work appears to be an ambivalent one. On the one hand film is used, like painting, as a filter through which the characters can express or navigate their emotions. On the other, modern media seem to be associated with loss and the inability to allow true communication. The internet in 'Carte postale de Lugano' is depicted as a limited tool: 'What you and I are trying to say is too cumbersome for the pixels, waves and bytes of modern media, it needs to be carried on foot, one word at a time, walking through the snow.'

SRL This theme is very important to me and I have thought a lot about it, particularly from the theoretical point of view. Part of my teaching at university involves the analysis of modern media and I have written various theoretical articles on the subject. I am at the same time attracted and disgusted by the myth of transparency and absolute fluidity that media like the internet encourage us to imagine, also by the idea of the immediacy and directness of transmission that takes place without any filters and is available to anybody. In my opinion, these notions are rather deceitful and this presumed transparency does not capture the truth. The truth is something extremely complex that, as the passage quoted in the question shows, cannot be conveyed through immediacy; nor can the entire content of one's heart suddenly be made available to others. It is an illusion or, at least, if we tried to do it, could cause lots of damage. I am in favour of mediation, which is why I have a critical attitude towards the new media, even though I do not reject them. I use the internet, write e-mails or text messages but I am aware of the false illusions they can create, illusions that are the complete opposite of what literature tries to achieve. Literature is mediation *par excellence*. Literature is never direct. Unlike testimonies or other forms of writing, it never leads you straight to a point: it gets you there only through a process of 'flânerie', a roundabout route.

KG/LR The importance of language and communication is clear in your work. Characters need language and you depict it often in nutritive terms. But to a certain extent communication appears fundamentally barred. Certain letters are not sent, others do not arrive and numerous characters find themselves unable to speak. To what extent could Le Sentier *be characterised as an attempt to pass beyond language since Alissa moves closer to happiness when her hold on language becomes looser, when she is unable to put things into words?*

SRL   There is certainly some truth in this observation. Alissa has regular meetings with her psychoanalyst and she talks a lot. She moves easily within discourse, and she manages to express her suffering through discourse. Discourse and suffering seem to be linked. However, when she has a relationship with a man who cannot express himself easily in words, Alissa is much happier. He makes her experience simpler things, enabling her to appreciate that part of her inner self that cannot be expressed verbally. This is obviously a form of recognition of the failure of language, something extremely painful for a writer, but perhaps also, paradoxically, a way of saying that if we writers stopped constantly searching for the right word that can never be found we would be happier too.

KG/LR If your characters explore notions of the incapacity of language, is this theme taken up also at narrative and authorial level? There appears to be an extended exploration of the possibilities of the printed medium in your novels as you play with typographical and literary conventions. You leave blank spaces in the layout of your pages, language at times breaks down as verbs disappear, sentences are not complete and ellipses speak volumes.

SRL   Yes, I tried to explore syntactical deconstruction in places in order to convey the complexity of human experience. Both syntactical and typographical devices are the result of this desire to portray moments of life in their multifariousness. Complexity cannot be rendered through a series of simple, straightforward sentences. These are integral aspects of my writing, particularly as I do not believe in the possibility of separating form and content. In my opinion, the things that I am trying to say can only be expressed through that kind of style.

KG/LR The influence of psychoanalysis is evident in your work. Do Avant *and* Le Sentier *also testify to the effect of contemporary French feminism on your writing? Your frequent use of italics to highlight problematic statements (for example the platitudes of the doctor to Mathilde) is reminiscent of Luce Irigaray, whilst your frequent references to the myth of Medusa make one think of the texts of Hélène Cixous.*

SRL I must say that although I have read the two writers you mention in your question, I don't feel really close to their way of thinking. What I like in them is the importance of the body and the unconscious, and the idea that the two are intimately connected. However, there is in me a certain aspiration towards the dominion of consciousness, towards discourse, towards dialectical rigour, towards rationality, which are usually considered male connotations and which belong to that universe Irigaray and Cixous want to eradicate. There is in me as a person, and in my writing, a deep contrast between the need to express the power of the unconscious and, at the same time, to structure my discourse in terms of consciousness. I don't know whether this tension is perceived by the reader but I feel it very acutely when I am writing. To simplify, we could say that both the 'male' pole and the 'female' pole cohabit in me.

KG/LR Mirrors and mirror images appear very frequently in your books and, talking of psychoanalysis, Lacan springs immediately to mind.

SRL In this case I entirely agree, mirrors are very important in my writing and my next book is constructed around a series of mirror images reflecting each other.

KG/LR The narrative view point in Le Sentier *and* Avant *is an insistently shifting one. At times the narrator is external to the characters and appears omnipotent and absolute. At other times the narrator hypothesises as if s/he were uncertain of events and thoughts. Elsewhere, the narrator disappears as the characters step in to narrate their own lives. To what extent do your narratives constitute an attempt to challenge the reader, encouraging us to evaluate our relationship to the written word?*

SRL   I don't like the idea of the reader as a passive consumer of a text but what I find interesting about your question is the reference to the omniscient narrator which, in my view, stresses the point we were making earlier, when talking of the coexistence of the male and female poles in my writing. On the one hand, we have the pole that tries to structure and order events, which becomes visible in a nineteenth-century style narrator (similar to the kind of narrator we find in Balzac's prose), on the other hand, the female pole linked to the idea of the stream of consciousness or psychoanalysis that is expressed by the characters' individual view points. I am never entirely satisfied with either of these two perspectives, hence the constant shifting of the narrative viewpoint. I am aware that the use of an omniscient narrator is outmoded and not entirely suitable for modern writing but at the same time I cannot hide my inner longing for structure.

(Bangor/Grandvaux, August – September 2005)

Translated by Laura Rotaro

History

Felicity Rash

Early British Travellers
to Switzerland 1611–1860

Until the late sixteenth century, most British travellers in Switzerland were passing through the country on their way to Italy or other southerly destinations. Then, with the growth in popularity of the 'European Grand Tour', increasing numbers were tempted to tarry longer, chiefly in towns and cities.[1] The number of British visitors to Switzerland grew steadily throughout the seventeenth and eighteenth centuries and the reasons for travelling there were various. Young men visited cities such as Geneva, Zürich, Bern and Basel for educational purposes or as diplomats, or to become tutors in well-to-do households; others sought refuge in Switzerland from religious persecution; other men and later, women, journeyed to Switzerland purely for the pleasure of seeing beautiful sights and learning about the land and its people. In the late eighteenth and early nineteenth centuries there was also an increase in visits from botanists and artists, chiefly landscape painters such as J. M. W. Turner. The Victorian age saw an increase in wealth among the British middle classes and Swiss resorts started to build facilities for the growing numbers of visitors.[2] The British played a major role in the development of mountaineering and other winter sports in Switzerland. The Alpine Club was founded in 1857 and the Englishman

1   See in particular John Wraight, *The Swiss and the British* (Salisbury: Michael Russell, 1987) and Jeremy Black, *The British Abroad. The Grand Tour in the Eighteenth Century* (Stroud: Alan Sutton Publishing, 1992), pp. 33–37.
2   Wraight, p. 34.

Edward Whymper was the first to conquer the Matterhorn in 1865. From the 1860s the British were influential in the introduction of skating, tobogganing and skiing in resorts such as St. Moritz, Davos and Zermatt, and until the early 1920s British tourists outnumbered those from other countries.[3]

In 1714 Abraham Stanyan wrote of a widespread ignorance of Switzerland and its people due to 'the Want of good Writers'. He claimed that most literature about the country could not be 'of general Use' because it was written in German,[4] although he omits any mention of the works of Coryat (1611), Burnet (1687) and Addison (1705). By the late eighteenth century the situation had improved considerably, the accounts of Willam Coxe (1779) and Helena Maria Williams (1789) being among the most informative. During the first half of the nineteenth century many well-known authors and poets visited Switzerland and it is largely the letters and memoirs of such people which are the main sources for this essay. Literary visitors included William Wordsworth (1790, 1820), Percy Bysshe Shelley (1814, 1816) and Mary Shelley (1814, 1816, 1840), Lord Byron (1816), Robert Southey (1817), Dorothy Wordsworth (1820), Thomas Lovell Beddoes (1835), John Ruskin (1835, 1841), Charles Dickens (1845, 1846) and George Eliot (1849–50). Those travelling to Switzerland after 1816 had a number of English-language guidebooks at their disposal: Henry Coxe's *Traveller's Guide* of 1816 was a major source for Gaglignani's *Traveller's Guide* of 1818, which also made use of Johann Gottfried Ebel's four-volume guide in German of 1804. The first organised tour to Switzerland was in 1818, arranged by Mr B. Emery of Charing Cross.[5] His tours were limited to six people. Mass tourism to Switzerland began with Thomas Cook's first organised tour in 1863, but as early as 1825,

---

3 ibid, p. 35.
4 Abraham Stanyan, *An account of Switzerland written in the year 1714* (Edinburgh: Hamilton, Balfour and Neill, 1756).
5 Wraight, p. 218.

William Hazlitt complained about the crowds of English visitors to be found in the Alps: 'Nor Alps not Apennines can keep them out / Nor fortified redoubt!'[6] Hazlitt criticised the proprietorial attitude of many British travellers:

> But the English abroad turn out of their way to see every pettifogging, huckstering object that they could see better at home, and are as fussy and fidgety, with their smoke-jacks and mechanical inventions among the Alps, as if they had brought Manchester and Sheffield in their pockets.[7]

This essay will present an overview of the experiences recounted by travellers to Switzerland before the advent of mass tourism during the 1860s: the first section will deal with descriptions of landscape, the second with accounts of the Swiss character and their way of life, and the third with the comments of various travellers on social differences in Switzerland.

1. *The Swiss landscape and its inhabitants*

In 1739, Horace Walpole, writing to Richard West, said of the Alps: 'Such uncouth rocks, and such uncomely inhabitants! My dear West, I hope I shall never see them again!'[8] Arriving in Switzerland almost a hundred years later, in 1835, John Ruskin felt that he had entered 'the Holy Land of my future work, and my true home in this world'.[9] This is not to say that the land and its mountains had become an earthly paradise in the course of a century, but there had

---

6   P. P. Howe (ed.), *The Complete Works of William Hazlitt*, 21 vols (London and Toronto: J. M. Dent, 1932), vol 10, p. 291.

7   Howe, vol 10, p. 290.

8   Mrs Paget Toynbee (ed.), *The Letters of Horace Walpole* (Oxford: The Clarendon Press, 1903), p. 40.

9   Wraight, p. 227.

been a significant change in the sensibilities and expectations of British
travellers to Switzerland, largely a result of having read Jean-Jacques
Rousseau's *Nouvelle Héloïse* (1761) and *Émile* (1762). During the
latter part of the eighteenth century Rousseau's works encouraged
those travelling to Switzerland for pleasure and enlightenment to
believe that they would find an unspoilt Arcadia in the Swiss mountains. Contemporary and later travellers, many of them authors in
their own right, undertook 'pilgrimages' to Rousseau's haunts in
what is now the Swiss canton of Neuchâtel, and to the scenes of his
Héloïse. James Boswell visited Rousseau in 1764, having read *Héloïse*
and *Émile*. He expected to find inspiration with Rousseau and in
the rugged mountain scenery which surrounded his home. He was
not disappointed with the 'Wild Philosopher' or his 'wild valley' (the
Val de Travers, near the village of Môtiers).[10] In 1816 Lord Byron
wrote that he had 'traversed all Rousseau's ground with the *Héloïse*
before me'.[11] He found nature and human beings existing in exemplary
harmony when he roamed the Alps and heard cows' bells, shepherds
playing pipes against a background of sublime scenery, confirming
'all that I have ever heard or imagined of a pastoral existence [...]
pure and unmixed – solitary, savage, and patriarchal: the effect I
cannot describe'.[12] From the early nineteenth century onwards, after
the turbulence of the French Revolution, the transience of human
endeavour became a popular literary theme. Lord Byron's *Childe
Harold* (Cantos III and IV) is an example of a poem which includes
this theme, stressing that nature and its beauty survive while human
efforts have short-lived consequences, the Alps exemplifying all that
endures.[13]

10   Frederick A. Pottle (ed.), *Boswell on the Grand Tour: Germany and Switzer-
     land, 1764* (London: Heinemann, 1953), p. 220f.
11   Rowland E. Prothero (ed.), *The Works of Lord Byron. Letters and Journals*
     (London: John Murray, 1899), vol III, p. 335.
12   ibid, p. 355.
13   H. J. C. Grierson (ed.), *Poems of Lord Byron* (London: Chatto & Windus,
     1923), p. x.

The idealisation of the Swiss mountains, however, often differed from the reality of early travel in Switzerland. Visitors to mountain regions frequently found primitive living conditions and a type of inhabitant that they considered uncivilised.[14] As one would expect, accommodation in towns and cities was superior, with an established *bourgeoisie* able to provide clean rooms and adequate food. The number of hotels named 'Bristol' in Swiss towns can be explained by the frequent visits to Switzerland during the late eighteenth century of Frederick Hervey, Bishop of Derry and fifth Earl of Bristol, who was renowned for staying only in the best hotels.[15] As far as rural areas were concerned, many accounts were less then glowing. William Hazlitt, for example, who visited Switzerland in 1825, depicts the Rhone as having a 'whitish muddy colour [...] very much as if [it] had been poured out of a washing-tub'. Hazlitt found the scenery of the Rhone Valley 'too barren and naked' and the forests gloomy – a good hiding-place for robbers.[16] Most accounts of the Alps extol their rugged beauty while at the same time recognising the dangers of the terrain and the changeable nature of the climate. Helena Maria Williams, for example, described the Reuss valley as a place 'where man is obliged to be continually at war with nature.[17] Lord Byron found the Simplon Pass magnificent, but thought that the Devil must have 'had a hand (or a hoof)' in the making of some of its rocks and ravines.[18] Percy Shelley wrote of ghosts of people who had been killed by avalanches roaming the

---

14 Hans Trümpy, *Schweizerdeutsche Sprache und Literatur im 17. und 18. Jahrhundert (auf Grund der gedruckten Quellen)* (= Schriften der Schweizerischen Gesellschaft für Volkskunde 36), (Basel: Krebs, 1955), p. 13.

15 Wraight, p. 34.

16 Howe, vol 10, p. 281f.

17 Helena Maria Williams, *A Tour in Switzerland; or, A View of the Present State of the Government and Manners of those Cantons: with Comparative Sketches of the Present State of Paris*, 2 vols (London: G. G. and J. Robinson, 1798), vol I, p. 154.

18 Prothero, p. 375.

mountains, 'their plaintive voices are still heard in stormy night, calling for succour from the peasants'.[19] Drawing upon his sources, Galignani's *Traveller's Guide* (1818) likens the mentality of the Swiss to the changeable climate of the country, feeling that the people cannot but be influenced by the vicissitudes of the Alpine climate:

> But the heavens are not always threatening, the lightning does not always flash in their eyes: immediately after the most dreadful tempest, the hemisphere clears itself by slow degrees, and becomes serene. The heads and the hearts of the Swiss are of a similar nature; kindness succeeds to anger, and generosity to the most brutal fury, as might be easily proved, not only from the records of history, but from recent fact.[20]

Book VI of William Wordsworth's *Prelude* includes one of the best-known poetic records of a trip to Switzerland. He described the route he walked in 1790 with Robert Jones over the Simplon pass from the Canton of Valais to Italy and, while we may not know how much poetic license influenced Wordsworth's scenic descriptions, it is clear that he found the going hard and some of his lodgings dreary.[21] In 1820 Wordsworth was accompanied on a tour of Switzerland by his wife Mary and his sister Dorothy, whose journals are a treasure-trove of information on the route, the landscape and the people that the travellers met. Also included are historical details, most notably of the relatively recent invasions by the French and the Russians, botanical information, and descriptions of local costumes, music and architecture. Dorothy also commented on the

19 E. B. Murray (ed.), *The Prose Works of Percy Bysshe Shelley*, (Oxford: Clarendon Press, 1993), vol. I, p. 197.

20 *Galignani's Traveller's Guide through Switzerland*, chiefly compiled from the much esteemed works of Ebel and Coxe [...] (Paris: Galignani, 1818), p. xv.

21 William Wordsworth, *The Prelude or Growth of a Poet's Mind*, ed. by Ernest de Selincourt (Oxford: Clarendon Press, 1926), p. 206.

political and legal systems of the cantons which she visited, and she was especially struck by the poverty of many mountain-dwellers. It is therefore extraordinary that Wraight barely mentions Dorothy Wordsworth in *The Swiss and the British* and omits her name from his index.

The commonest sentiment expressed by early British travellers throughout Switzerland was, as one would expect, that the mountains, the Alps more so than the Jura, were breathtakingly beautiful. Percy Shelley was so overwhelmed on first seeing the Alps in 1817 that he felt his imagination being put to the test:

> Their immensity staggers the imagination, and so far surpasses all conceptions, that it requires an effort of the understanding to believe that they indeed form a part of the earth.[22]

Dorothy Wordsworth more than once commented that the beauty of Switzerland is hard to imagine until one sees it for oneself and that it would be a very insensitive person who were not touched by the natural wonders found there:

> [...] standing at the further end of a wide oblong hollow, surrounded by granite pikes, snow pikes, masses of granite, cool, black, motionless shadows, and sparkling sunshine it is not possible for the dullest imagination to be unmoved. [23]

Dorothy adopts a tone of self-deprecation when she claims that she cannot attempt to describe the Rhine Falls at Schaffhausen because 'Coxe and other travellers have done it better than I',[24] yet her ensuing portrayal of the Falls is detailed and impassioned, evoking the awe and fear which filled her when she first caught sight of them:

22 Murray, p. 196
23 Dorothy Wordsworth, *The Journals of Dorothy Wordsworth*, ed. by Ernest de Selincourt (London: Macmillan, 1941), vol. II, p. 262.
24 ibid, p. 89; the Coxe referred to may have been William Coxe (1779) or Henry Coxe (1816).

> It is impossible even to *remember* (therefore how should I enable any one to imagine?) the power of the dashing, and of the sounds – the breezes – the dancing dizzy sensations – and the exquisite beauty of the colours! The whole stream falls like liquid emeralds – a solid mass of translucent green hue – or, in some parts, the green appears through a thin covering of snow-like foam. Below, in the ferment and hurly-burly, drifting snow, the masses resembling collected snow, mixed with sparkling green billows. [25]

Helena Williams's accomplished portrayal of the Rhine Falls gives voice to the Romantic notion that the mind is elevated and ennobled by the contemplation of Nature's wonders: 'Such objects appear to belong to immortality; they call the musing mind from all its little cares and vanities'.[26]

While repeatedly comparing the Swiss Alps to the British Lake District and Scotland, Dorothy Wordsworth hovers between delight at the natural beauty she encounters and fear of uncontrollable natural forces, especially of the violent August thunder-storms that appear to be following the travellers on their way. Dorothy and her companions were ever aware that Nature can be both beautiful and dangerous, and also uncomfortable to members of the human race. During one storm, Dorothy is dismayed at the way in which the lightning invades her bedroom, simultaneously illuminating the mountains, which seem alarmingly close to her bedroom window:

> I shall never forget the awfulness of the blaze in my bedroom, that succeeded total darkness and shewed me the mountain side apparently close to the window; what peels of thunder in that pent-up valley! and what a continual roaring of the river![27]

In 1850, on the other hand, George Eliot noted that reports of the dangers of the Swiss mountains were apt to be exaggerated by the

25 Dorothy Wordsworth, p. 90.
26 Helena Williams, vol I, p. 61.
27 Dorothy Wordsworth, p. 180.

English news media, and that she had heard of no wolves descending from the mountains to devour the inhabitants of villages.[28]

A major preoccupation of Dorothy Wordsworth's was that man was increasing his control over Nature. To her the Valais was a place of 'natural solitude [...] unmastered by the equalising contrivances of men'; in one place she saw carts and carriages which 'called to mind the stir and traffic of the world in a place which might have been destined for perpetual solitude, where the thunder of heaven, the rattling of Avalanches, and the roaring of winds and torrents seemed to be the only turbulent sounds, that had a right to take the place of the calm and silence which surrounded us'.[29] Similarly, Helena Williams was struck by the smallness of 'fleeting man' against a background of the 'vast, eternal, uncontrollable grandeur' of nature. Like many travellers, she had anticipated the beauty of the Alps long before she saw them herself: 'How often had the idea of those stupendous mountains filled my heart with enthusiastic awe!'[30] For Percy Shelley it was easy to comprehend that Switzerland's 'sublime mountains' would be a fitting homeland for a hero such as William Tell and 'a fit cradle for a mind aspiring to high adventure and heroic deeds'.[31]

2. *The Swiss character and way of life*

Over the centuries the Swiss have been described as simple, frugal, honest, serious, phlegmatic, reserved, brave, polite, industrious, meticulous, neat, well-dressed, contented, home-loving, stubborn, proud (especially of their mountains), musical and mercenary to

28 J. W. Cross (ed.), *George Eliot's Life as Related in Her Letters and Journals* (Edinburgh & London: William Blackwood and Sons, 1885), p. 245f.

29 Dorothy Wordsworth, pp. 263, 262.

30 Helena Williams, vol I, p. 63.

31 Murray, p. 197.

the point of being cut-throat. Dorothy Wordsworth's account of her visit to Switzerland in 1820 attests to each one of these qualities, many but not all of which are already recounted in travellers' accounts from the seventeenth century onwards. In 1739, for example, Thomas Gray commented on the 'happy and lively countenances' of the inhabitants of Geneva, and the fact that people were busy and well-dressed.[32] Lord Byron commented on the close-knit and happy families that he met in Switzerland, writing that the peasants were rich and 'the cows superb'; writing of the Canton of Bern he echoed what many visitors claimed for the entire country, namely, that it was 'famous for Cheese, liberty, property, and no taxes'.[33] Percy Shelley was one of the few visitors bold enough to verbalise a negative generalisation, namely, that the Swiss were 'a people slow of comprehension and of action'; they were, however, 'unfit for slavery' and therefore always ready to defend their freedom against invaders.[34]

While many early reports of Switzerland stress characteristics common to all Swiss men and women, some diversity is also recorded. Mostly this is a matter of differences between inhabitants of different regions, with mountain folk generally deemed to be slower of wit, ruder, dirtier, and poorer in health than townsfolk. The upper Valais is the most frequently derided region.[35] William Coxe characterised the population of this area as lazy and negligent, believing the Valaisans' indolence to be the cause of their unwholesome water and therefore of their tendency to suffer from goitres (or 'wens'). Coxe also believed the goitres to be caused in part by moral flaws; for example, he accused the Valaisans of neglecting their

32 Wraight, p. 164.
33 Prothero, p. 356.
34 Murray, p. 197.
35 Thomas Martyn, *Sketch of a Tour through Switzerland* (London: G. Kearsley, 1787), p. 79; Robert Bakewell, *Travels [...] in Switzerland and Auvergne in 1820, 1821 and 1822*, 2 vols (London: Longman, Hurst, Rees, Orme, and Brown, 1823), p. 218.

children.[36] The dwellings in the Ticino are described in much travel literature as dirty and crumbling, and the people as lazy and prone to drunkenness.[37] More than one author states that the Ticinese areas situated closer to the German language-boundary are the cleanest. The Canton of Uri is mentioned as being plagued with poverty and beggars on the one hand, and benefitting from the commerce brought from traffic across the St. Gothard Pass on the other.[38]

As early as 1685 Bishop Gilbert Burnet commented on the propriety and industry of the citizens of Bern, especially of the women:

> The men are generally sincere, but heavy, they think it necessary to correct the moisture of the Air with liberal entertainments [...]. The women are generally imploied in their domestick affairs [...] and [...] so much amused with the management at home [...] that made them sleep well [...] nor did they know what Amours were.[39]

Bern is also one of the cantons claimed by Abraham Stanyan to be inhabited by people who are particularly polite, the others being Fribourg and Solothurn. Stanyan believed that the proximity of the French border influenced manners and dress in these cantons in a positive way and reduced the rate of drunkenness among men.[40] Writing about the food he ate on his 1825 journey, William Hazlitt

36 William Coxe, *Sketches of the Natural, Civil and Political State of Swisserland in a series of letters to William Melmouth, Esq.* (London: J. Dodsley, 1779), p. 265f.

37 Frederic Shoberl, *Switzerland in Miniature; Containing a Description of the Character, Manners, Customs, Diversions, Dress, &c. of the People of that Country* (London: R. Ackermann, 1827), p. 272f.

38 Charles J. Latrobe, *The Alpenstock; or, sketches of Swiss scenery and manners* (London: R. B. Seeley and W. Burnside, 1829), p. 74; Shoberl, p. 215f.

39 Gilbert Burnet, *Some letters containing an account of what seemed most remarkable in Switzerland, Italy, &c Rotterdam* (Amsterdam: Peter Savouret and W. Fenner, 1687), p. 19; cf. George Eliot's letter to the Brays of October 1849, quoted in Cross, p. 230.

40 Stanyan, pp. 137–39.

declared that the Swiss 'have not the art here of adulterating every thing. You find the same things as in England, served up in the same plain manner, but in greater plenty, and generally speaking, of a better and more wholesome quality'.[41] Philip Stanhope, however, accused the Swiss of 'entire ignorance of the first rudiments of cookery'.[42] Geneva is the canton to be most praised in early travel literature as clean, civilised and liberal, 'a model in miniature of the country we were about to visit'.[43] Stanyan maintained that the Genevans were sensitive to the fact that the French despised all Swiss people and thought them dull-witted. This caused Genevans to 'look upon it as a real misfortune to be Switzers, and [...] not care to pass for such'.[44] According to Frederic Shoberl, the man from Schwyz was modest, upright, sincere, fearless and 'not subject to any kind of servitude'; 'he gathers in peace the fruit of his labour, and freely enjoys it; thus cheerfulness prevails in his character, and frankness in his looks and language'. The people of Einsiedeln, on the other hand, were criticised as superstitious, idle and inclined to begging, probably due to the fact that they were able to profit from the good will of pilgrims. While the Fribourgeois were especially devout, Shoberl stated that he could find nothing to say at all about Schaffhausen.[45]

The Galignani guide-book of 1818 mentions a change in the behaviour of the Swiss people as a whole since the appearance of early written accounts:

41 Howe, vol 10, p. 285f.
42 Philip Stanhope, *Letters from Switzerland*. Unpublished, Karlsruhe: printed by W. Hasper, 1833, p. 96.
43 William Liddiard, *A Three Months' Tour in Switzerland and France* (London: Smith, Elder and Co., 1832), p. 48; compare Joseph Addison, *Remarks on Several Parts of Italy and Switzerland, &c. in the Year 1701, 1702, 1703* (London: Jacob Tonson, 1705), p. 503.
44 Stanyan, p. 128.
45 Shoberl, pp. 153, 157, 245, 285.

> The manners of the Swiss peasants are still frank and honest, but less rough and unpolished than they formerly were. The gentry and burghers have lost some of their original simplicity of character, and, occasionally affect refinement, and give way to dissipation. [46]

It may be assumed that this transformation was partly due to an increase in tourism. Many authors wrote of the effects upon the Swiss of exposure to foreigners and their habits as a result of foreign travellers visiting Switzerland and of Swiss citizens, mostly mercenaries in foreign military service, living abroad. Foreign influence was one of the motivations for the introduction of sumptuary laws common in many Swiss towns: 'excesses in apparel' and the 'consumption of foreign commodities' were said to cause young people to live beyond their means and to affect the Swiss balance of trade negatively.[47] It should be noted, however, that it was mercenaries returning from France rather than British travellers who were commonly blamed for influencing Swiss dress and manners.[48] Later authors also wrote of a 'lamentable change' in the Swiss and of increased drunkenness, largely due to the influence of both foreign visitors to Switzerland and to the Swiss travelling abroad. Philip Stanhope quotes a French author as claiming that 'la Suisse touche à sa fin', while Charles Latrobe felt that the moral degeneration of the Swiss was the unsurprising result of the French invasion following the Revolution. Peasants were deemed to have become particularly cut-throat as a result of tourism and no longer 'the simple, virtuous, patriarchal race that their forefathers were'.[49] In William Coxe's travel account we find recorded a particularly interesting conversation with a Leukerbad resident who told Coxe that the accommodation at the Baths was kept simple so as to prevent the

46 Galignani, p. xiv.
47 Stanyan, p. 166f.; cf. Addison, p. 499f., who also suggested that foreign influence might cause the Swiss to lose their 'Military Roughness'.
48 ibid, p. 135.
49 Stanhope, p. 81, Latrobe, pp. 324–28.

'concourse of strangers' which might 'serve to introduce luxury among the inhabitants, and insensibly destroy the simplicity of manner, for which the Vallaisans are so remarkably distinguished'; Coxe wondered 'how far the ignorance of a people can contribute to their true felicity?'[50]

Physical courage is possibly the oldest positive quality to be attributed to the majority of Swiss men, due to the excellent reputation of mercenaries and the Swiss Guard. Abraham Stanyan wrote in 1714 that the warlike nature of the Swiss was already famous within the Roman Empire:

> There is no one quality so universally allowed to the Switzers as that of valour [...] Livy and Caesar speak of them in their writings as a brave warlike people; and they have ever since kept up that character in the world. [51]

Patriotism was allied to bravery as a Swiss trait and associated in 1764 by Oliver Goldsmith with the harsh lifestyle of many Swiss mountain people: 'Thus every good his native wilds impart / Imprints the patriot passion on his heart'.[52]

Although Dorothy Wordsworth also acknowledged the 'savage fearlessness' of the Swiss, her first impresssion on arriving in Schaffhausen from Germany was that Swiss innkeepers were more welcoming and helpful than their German counterparts. Dorothy preferred travelling on foot, and we must be thankful for this because she would have observed many fewer interesting details of the land and its people had she travelled in a carriage. Her overall impression of the Swiss people in both French-speaking and German-speaking Switzerland, was one of cheerfulness, civility and interest in visitors.

50 William Coxe, p. 231.
51 Stanyan, p. 119; cf. Oliver Goldsmith, 'The Traveller: or, A Prospect of Society', in *Collected Works of Oliver Goldsmith* (Oxford: Clarendon Press, 1966), vol. IV, pp. 235–69.
52 Goldsmith, p. 257; cf. George Eliot in Cross, p. 212.

Dorothy writes of two shopkeepers in Simpeln as having 'simple undisguised inquisitiveness', and as being keener to ask questions of the travellers than answer them. She considered the Ticino to be a region of Italy and found the people there 'not gay as in some parts of Switzerland'.[53]

In the course of her journey through Switzerland, Dorothy repeatedly encountered hospitality, kindness and civility.[54] Peasants were particularly friendly:

> They addressed me with kindly smiles; and often I thought I could have no fears, except from the tremendous powers of nature, if wandering alone among these simple people.[55]

It appears that Dorothy was looking for the best in everyone she met, and she remembers William speaking of her '"delusion"' when on one occasion she thought of a Swiss girl's 'sociable kindness' as having 'proceeded from pure good-will'. As Dorothy read some travel accounts before leaving home, we might assume a certain bias in her own account, stemming from a view of Switzerland and the Swiss acquired prior to her departure. Dorothy was not, however, incapable of recognising less agreeable settings and situations. She noticed, for example, that some Catholic Swiss were less inclined to treat Protestant tourists graciously, her guide remarking on their arrival in Lungern that the local people 'would neither give nor sell anything to us Protestants except in the regular way of trade. They would do nothing for us out of goodwill'.[56]

In 1714 Abraham Stanyan wrote of the 'sound and clear judgement' of the Swiss and their 'dexterity in the management of affairs'.[57] Dorothy Wordsworth saw the Swiss as naturally frugal and well

---

53 Dorothy Wordsworth, pp.113, 87, 259, 267, 192, 193.
54 ibid, pp. 97, 102, 121, 134.
55 ibid, p. 122; cf. George Eliot's letters in Cross, p. 234.
56 Dorothy Wordsworth, pp. 278, 136.
57 Stanyan, p. 125.

organised, with every inch of land being put to use for profit, as in the following example:

> A woman was leading two goats and a kid by the same string along the line of a low hedge, clipped as with shears. [...] With what patient industry do these people avail themselves of every benefit that a kindly climate affords! [58]

Dorothy Wordsworth noticed that, as far as development of tourism was concerned, the Swiss were very quick to recognise opportunities for making money. Wherever the Wordsworth party roamed in 1820 they would be greeted by people, often children, offering to act as guides or to sell them fruit, flowers or souvenirs. Price inflation tended to follow an increase in the number of British tourists in a particular town or village, and Dorothy recorded both good and bad experiences in this respect; in particular she remembered a meal which cost a mere 12 'batzen' as 'a proof that this town is not frequently the halting-place of the English'.[59] A few years later Charles Latrobe noted as an example of Swiss entrepreneurship that the mountain 'vacheries' exported most of their best cheese to Russia: 'Wenig mühe und viel profit (little trouble and much profit) is the saying among these peasants'.[60] By 1833 Philip Stanhope felt it appropriate to quote the proverb 'Point d'argent, point de Suisses' and wonder if it could be true that the Swiss would do nothing at all unless they were paid for it. He further claimed that the Swiss in some respects failed to live up to their reputations as good entrepreneurs, giving as an example the lack of good roads to facilitate trade and tourism.[61] Like many a modern tourist, William Coxe thought that the expense of travelling (he quotes the high price of hiring a horse) in Switzerland was outweighed by the delights of the scenery.[62]

58 Dorothy Wordsworth, p. 97.
59 ibid, pp. 175, 98, 150, 142.
60 Latrobe, p. 227.
61 Stanhope, p. 71f.
62 William Coxe, p. 155.

Oliver Goldsmith, who visited Switzerland in 1755, saw the country, with its poor soil and harsh climate, as representative of all 'barren states'; to him it was a land where the people were contented and cheerful despite difficult living conditions and a lack of material luxury: 'even here, content can spread a charm / Redress the clime, and all its rage disarm'.[63] The Swiss peasant farmer is romanticised by Goldsmith as dignified in his simple existence; unaware of any richer lifestyle and satisfied with his lot, he is the 'monarch of a shed':

> He sees his little lot, the lot of all;
> Sees no contiguous palace rear its head
> To shame the meanness of his humble shed;
> [...] But calm, and bred in ignorance and toil,
> Each wish contracting, fits him to the soil.
> Chearful at morn he wakes from short repose,
> Breasts the keen air, and carrols as he goes.[64]

In the nineteenth century Dorothy Wordsworth was similarly impressed by the Swiss way of performing the hardest of tasks with great cheer and infinite patience; she also noted that most inns and private houses, from the grandest of buildings to the humblest of mountain huts, were clean and tidy; even the dunghills were neatly built:

> The vicinity of dunghills to the balconies and to the other pleasing contrivances for out-of-doors enjoyment in hours of rest, beside the farm-houses, did not, however accord with our English notions, yet we could not but admire the neatness with which they were constructed, as by rule and measure, no stray litter overpassing the boundary line.

The proximity of neat dunghills to human habitation, the precision with which even the contents of a farmyard are measured, and flower-

---

63 Goldsmith, pp. 256–59.
64 ibid, p. 256.

pots in windows are two of the features of Swiss farms that strike
visitors to Switzerland even today.[65]

In his fascinating essay 'Hot and Cold', William Hazlitt draws
upon his experiences of travelling in Switzerland and Italy in order to
compare inhabitants of northern and southern latitudes. Switzerland
is cold and the people clean; Italy is hot and the people dirty ('they
have a dread of ablutions and absterions, almost amounting to
hydrophobia'). The humours of the 'Helvetian boor' creep 'through
his veins like the dank mists along the sides of his frozen mountains';
he is 'endued' to the climate because 'the phlegmatic blood of their
German ancestors is poured down the valleys of the Swiss like water,
and iced in its progress'. Everything in his land is therefore 'purified
and filtered'. In Brig, 'neat-handed Phyllises' wash the caterpillars
from their vegetables and scour their pails until no stain is left. Hazlitt
therefore dismisses the remarks of a shopkeeper in Vevey, who had
told him that Protestants are cleaner than Catholics, as the meticulous
inhabitants of Brig are Catholic. Hazlitt's 'Notes of a Journey through
France and Italy', however, gives an altogether more differentiated account of the Rhone valley; he characterises Sion as 'one of the dirtiest
and least comfortable towns on the road', its inn deserving the epithet
'*simplex munditiis*', and Martigny as desolate.[66]

However 'cold-blooded' the Swiss may have seemed to some travellers, a large number commented on their love of song and dance.
Lord Byron admired the singing and dancing of village people, such
as he observed in Brienz: '[t]he airs are so wild and original, and
at the same time of great sweetness'. He was kept awake one night
by 'pretty music and excellent Waltzing', which he remarked was
performed by 'none but peasants' and executed better than by any
English person ('the English can't Waltz, never could, nor ever will').[67]
Dorothy Wordsworth was impressed by the habit of mountain guides

65 Dorothy Wordsworth, pp. 273–75, 117, 126, 103, 104.
66 Howe, vol 12, p. 169.
67 Prothero, p. 361.

singing hymns or 'pensive songs' as they walked,[68] and Charles Latrobe described yodelling as 'clear, strong, and sonorous tones' that could carry a great distance.[69] This is, no doubt, what William Liddiard meant when he said of the strange contrapuntal music made by peasant women that it 'seemed as if the music had been borrowed from the mountain echoes'.[70] It was the famous 'Ranz des Vaches' (the literal meaning of which is 'cows' tails') which impressed Lord Byron. These French-Swiss folk songs fascinated many a traveller, and William Hazlitt told of how Swiss peasants were filled with 'Heimweh' when they heard them:

> [...] which [...] when its well-known sound is heard, does not merely recal [sic] to them the idea of their country, but has associated with it a thousand nameless ideas, numberless touches of private affection, of early hope, romantic adventure, and national pride, all which rush in (with mingled currents) to swell the tide of fond remembrance, and make them languish or die for home.[71]

This sentiment is doubtless the 'maladie du pays' described earlier by William Coxe, who explained that Swiss troops in French service were forbidden from singing 'Ranz des Vaches' as these caused in the hearers a 'patriotic regret' which often occasioned desertion; Coxe believed that people whose homes were in mountainous areas, such as the Swiss, the Scots and the 'Biscayans' were more prone to 'maladie du pays' than other folk.[72]

As with Swiss music, the standard language and dialects of Switzerland were a matter of great interest and, occasionally, confusion to early British travellers. Most adduced that the country was divided into French- and German-speaking areas, Italian and

68 Dorothy Wordsworth, pp. 273–75.
69 Latrobe, p. 32.
70 Liddiard, pp. 107–09.
71 Howe, vol 8, p. 35.
72 William Coxe, pp. 327, 329.

Rhaeto-Romansch rarely being mentioned as Swiss national languages, except by Frederic Shoberl, who provides a good account of the linguistic situation in the Canton of Graubünden.[73] In 1714 Abraham Stanyan explained that French is used in Bern, Fribourg and Solothurn 'among the Better sort', that few German-speaking Swiss can write German, and that the use of French has led to an undesirable 'freedom of behaviour' and 'frivolity of dress' in both men and women.[74] The chief concern of many early visitors to the German-speaking cantons was whether their hosts would speak English or, if not English, French. Few British visitors could understand German and even fewer any Swiss-German dialect (apart from Charles Latrobe and Louis Agassiz, the latter providing a list of 'useful phrases'). Even those tourists who were not proficient in German criticised its sounds and complained that the dialects and standard language as used in Switzerland were equally unintelligible and harsh sounding. Both Mary and Percy Shelley described Swiss German as 'barbarous', and for Thomas Martyn it was 'bastard German' (he also called Swiss French 'corrupt').[75] Marianne Baillie, who visited Switzerland in the early nineteenth century, described the language she heard thus:

> It is not to be told how disagreeably the German language grated upon our ears in passing through these cantons; after the mellifluous harmony of the Italian, and even compared with the French, it was doubly intolerable. Our own is harsh enough, in the opinion of foreigners; yet I can with difficulty imagine any thing so bad as German.[76]

73 Shoberl, p. 230f.
74 Stanyan, p. 148.
75 Jane Robinson (ed.), *Unsuitable for Ladies: Mary Shelley: 'History of a Six Weeks' Tour'* (Oxford: OUP, 1994), p. 60, Murray, p. 198; Martyn, p. 74.
76 Marianne Baillie, *First impressions on a tour upon the continent in the summer of 1818, through parts of France, Italy, Switzerland, the borders of Germany and a part of Flanders* (London: John Murray, 1819), p. 317.

John Carne, on the other hand, praised the Glarus dialect of a group of women who 'laughed, romped, made their bargains, and talked their soft sweet mountain German with infinite melody of accent'.[77] The German Swiss predilection for diminutive suffixes, while found quaint and pretty by some visitors, was thought ludicrous by Frederic Shoberl:

> A singularity of this latter dialect is the frequent use of diminutive terminations. Names and nouns proper, verbs, pronouns and all, are susceptible of these forms, which are sometimes employed very unreasonably. An athletic herdsman, for instance, is not John or Martin, but little John, or little Martin, even though he were above six feet high; and he will talk about his little eye, his little leg, or his little hand.[78]

Communication and politeness are chiefly a matter of language, and nowadays the Swiss have a reputation for being both polite and very formal.[79] While many early travellers appear to have found the Swiss less than polite for not trying hard enough to communicate with them in English, William Coxe was 'mortified' that he knew no Swiss German, as he felt that his hosts had many matters of interest to explain to him.[80] Dorothy Wordsworth lamented that she could not communicate in their own language with some Swiss women to whom she presented some needles, and when in Andermatt she and her companions saw a group of girls playing with a cat and they 'noticed the cat for the Maidens' sake; and they seemed to understand

77 John Carne, *Letters from Switzerland and Italy, during a late tour* (London: Henry Colburn, 1834), p. 63.
78 Shoberl, p. 42.
79 Felicity Rash, 'Linguistic Politeness and Greetings Rituals in German-speaking Switzerland', *Dialectology of Swiss German* (a special issue of *linguistik-online* 2003/04, ed. by Beat Siebenhaar), http://www.linguistik-online. org/20_04.
80 William Coxe, p. 43.

our motive as well as city breeding could have taught them'.[81] In each of these cases the Swiss are described as meeting their visitors at least halfway, and, as noted above, Dorothy Wordsworth in particular was inclined to look for the best in everyone she met. Some earlier travellers, however, complained of hostile receptions. Writing in the seventeenth century, John Evelyn told of the hostility with which he had been met in mountain regions, most notably on the Simplon pass, where his companion's dog was accused of killing a goat. In towns, however, such as Sion, St. Maurice and Geneva, where he spent six weeks in 1646 recovering from smallpox, Evelyn was greeted with civility. Percy Shelley wrote of the 'brutal rudeness' of some Swiss travelling companions during his visit of 1817. They were 'of the meanest class, smoked prodigiously, and were exceedingly disgusting'. Shelley's English friend, S***, was provoked by their rudeness and incomprehensible language to hit one man. In 1825 William Hazlitt noted a lack of good manners in Geneva and put this down to the fact that the Genevan government was republican (in general travellers found Genevans to be polite).[82]

While some Swiss were rude to foreign visitors, their manners towards one another fascinated many travellers. In the seventeenth century, Gilbert Burnet gave a rare insight into the different greeting habits of men and women:

> [...] their Women not only do not converse familiarly with Men; except those of their near Kindred, but even on the Streets do not make any returns to the Civility of Strangers, for it is only Strangers that put off their Hats to Women; but they make no courtesies; and here as in all Switzerland Women are not saluted, but the Civility is expressed by taking them by the Hand.[83]

---

81 Dorothy Wordsworth, pp. 129, 187, (cf. p. 112).
82 John Evelyn, *The Diaries and Correspondence of John Evelyn*, ed. by William Bray (London: George Routledge, n.d.), pp. 156–59; Murray, p. 199; Howe, vol 10, p. 295.
83 Gilbert, p. 44f.

Charles Latrobe described the modes of greeting and forms of address which were in general use in nineteenth-century Switzerland. He noted the formality with which apparently simple folk addressed one another:

> Englishmen, who are accustomed to no mode of greeting in their own country, but the dry and unmeaning, *How do you do!* cannot fail to be struck with the simple and patriarchal modes of salutation in the Swiss-German Cantons. In the Canton of Berne, high and low, rich and poor exclaim when they meet you, *Gott grüss'euch* (God salute you) – *Gott behüte euch* (May God shield you), or *Guten abend geb-euch Gott* (May God give you a good evening). In the Forest Cantons, a mode of greeting, yet more striking, is usual; the one, touches his cap, and exclaims *Gelobt sey Jesus Christus* (Jesus Christ be praised), to which the other responds, *In ewigkeit, Amen* (For ever and ever, Amen)! These are the relics of simple and delightful days, which are but too quickly fading away, even amongst the mountains.[84]

Latrobe further wrote that even simple folk, often members of village and town councils, addressed one another formally (e.g. *Der Herr Kleiner Raths-Herr, Der Ober Lieutenant, Herr Statthalter*), and in 1833 Louis Agassiz wrote of the custom of bowing, interpreting this as an act intended to put the addressee at ease.[85]

As well as being impressed with the way in which the Swiss communicated with one another privately and in more formal settings, British travellers praised the Swiss system of government, which worked according to long-established democratic principles. Since the Middle Ages, Switzerland has been known as a land of the free and Wilhelm Tell as the initiator of that freedom. In 1701, Joseph

---

84 Latrobe, pp. 89–90.

85 ibid, p. 337; Louis Agassiz, *A journey to Switzerland and pedestrian tours in that country; including a sketch of its history, and of the manners and customs of its inhabitants* (London: Smith, Elder and Co, 1833), p.159, cf. also Dorothy Wordsworth, p. 148.

Addison applauded the political organisation of the confederated cantons as follows:

> It is very wonderful to see such a Knot of Governments, that are so divided among themselves in Matters of Religion, maintain so uninterrupted an Union and Correspondence, that no one of 'em is for Invading the Rights of another [...]. This, I think, must be chiefly ascrib'd to the Nature of the People, and the Constitution of their Governments. Were the Swiss animated by Zeal and Ambition, some or other of their States would immediately break in upon the rest [...]. But as the Inhabitants of these Countries are naturally of a Phlegmatick Temper, if any of their Leading Members have more Fire and Spirit than comes to their Share, it is quickly temper'd by the Coldness and Moderation of the rest that sit at the Helm with 'em.[86]

He added that the Alps are the worst place on earth for making conquests. Thomas Lovell Beddoes, who had more of an insider's view of Switzerland than that of an average traveller, having studied medicine in Zürich, wrote a number of poems in German, one of which, 'Auf den Neujahrstag 1839', tells of the oath on the Grütli meadow which secured for the Swiss their freedom from the Hapsburgs; in his brief poem *An den Grossen Rath*, he also felt justified in criticising the government of Zürich for being filled with discord.[87]

3. *Social commentary*

It was not uncommon for early British visitors to Switzerland to believe that they were entering a land of liberty and equality. Many had read in advance the accounts of other travellers and on their arrival felt their expectations to be confirmed. William Coxe, for example, wrote of his feelings on arrival in Schaffhausen: 'I have

---

86 Addison, p. 496f.
87 H. W. Donner, *The Works of Thomas Lovell Beddoes* (London: OUP, 1935), pp. 143f., 150.

great pleasure in breathing the air of liberty: every person here has apparently the mien of content and satisfaction'; according to Coxe the Swiss possessed a 'natural frankness, and particular tone of equality' which arose from their 'consciousness of their independence'; he also noted that the 'natural equality' of the Swiss caused people to talk together who would be prevented from doing so in England due to social distinctions.[88] Few British travellers, however, were convinced that life was equally comfortable for all Swiss people; most realised that there was a firm social structure in the cities, and that rural dwellers were less advantaged than townsfolk in many respects. Abraham Stanyan, who lived in the city of Bern for eight years during the early eighteenth century, specifies three classes of Swiss society: the peasants, the gentry and vassals, and the citizens. He differentiates between 'aristocratical' and democratic cantons, Bern and Luzern being 'aristocratical'. Swiss peasants are adjudged by Stanyan to be industrious, hardy, 'bold in action, and obedient in discipline', apart from the peasants of Vaud, who he claims are 'accused of laziness, and of being given to stealing' because of the 'goodness of their soil'; he classes the vassals and gentry as the 'least happy' of all Swiss people, as they play only a minor role in government and have few sources of income, hence they have to seek their fortune in foreign service. Swiss citizens may be tradesmen, merchants, 'pen-men', and military men who have served abroad; the latter are the most esteemed of all citizens because they are the most polite and because 'the trade of arms is reckoned here the most honourable'.[89]

Visitors to mountain areas encountered chiefly the peasant class, and, while there was a tendency to sentimentalise the nature of the Swiss peasant, particularly after the works of Rousseau had made their impact on Western society, most travellers recognised that the poorer Swiss had a very hard life and often suffered as a result

88 William Coxe, pp. 6, 43, 74.
89 Stanyan, pp. 128f., 130, 132.

of social injustice. In Chapter 12, Book IV of his *Modern Painters*, entitled 'The Mountain Gloom', John Ruskin examines the effect of the 'sadness of the hills' upon the human heart and asks how mankind has benefitted from the 'instruction of the hills'; he judges the Canton of Valais near Martigny to have the purest mountain character, no war having drawn a veil between the mountains and the human soul, 'no contradicting voice [...] had confused their ministries of sound, or broken their pathos of silence'. Ruskin finds, however, that the beauty of the mountains means nothing to the peasants who live there. The paintings of happy peasants, 'in gay ribands and white bodices, singing sweet songs, and bowing gracefully to the picturesque crosses', which are sold in Paris and London, portray a 'False Ideal'. He claims that the money made selling such 'simulcrae' would be better spent putting songs into the mouths of existing peasants. Ruskin's own picture of peasant life, painted in well-chosen words, is of poverty, torpor, 'gloomy foulness' and 'anguish of soul'. The people who dwell in peasant huts, though surrounded by scenery that visitors find beautiful, 'do not understand so much as the name of beauty, or of knowledge':

> Love, patience, hospitality, faith, – these are the things they know. [...] For them, there is neither hope nor passion of spirit; for them neither advance nor exultation. Black bread, rude roof, dark night, laborious day, weary arm at sunset; and life ebbs away. No books, no thoughts, no attainments, no rest; except only sometimes a little sitting in the sun under the church wall, as the bell tolls thin and far in the mountain air [...][90]

Little comment was made on social inequalities in either rural or urban areas, but Helena Williams wrote briefly of the exploitation of craftspeople:

90   E. T. Cook and Alexander Wedderburn (eds), *The Works of John Ruskin* (London: George Allen, 1904), vol IV, pp. 418, 385, 385, 390, 388f.

[...] in vain the father of a family may cultivate his field of flax [...] in vain his wife may spin, his infants turn the wheel which winds the thread, and he himself weave the woof; the web when woven is not at his disposition.[91]

Louis Simond accused the Bernese nobility of 'pride and stateliness' and of keeping the citizens at a great distance; their wives and daughters were reluctant to mix with merchant families at balls and public occasions.[92] The Catholic Church was also criticised by Charles Latrobe for exacerbating social problems and for failing to improve 'the moral and physical condition of a poor ignorant peasantry'; Latrobe wrote of well-fed priests who would take money 'bestowed as a donation for whitewashing their souls' that might have been better spent on food, clothing and soap.[93] Many British travellers to Switzerland linked poverty to ignorance and remarked upon the tendency of mainly peasant people towards superstition and belief in witchcraft. Frederic Shoberl records that a woman was put to death for witchcraft as late as 1782.[94] Latrobe tells of old people who remember the 'Nachtvölkli' (night spirits) visiting the houses of their parents at night with 'good natured offers of assistance'. This author bewails the loss of traditional beliefs: 'Alas! alas! we live in a sad matter-of-fact age, where incredulity is much more fashionable than that amiable and unhesitating credence in matters like these'. Philip

91 Williams, vol I, p. 104.
92 Louis Simond, *Switzerland, or, a Journal of a Tour and Residence in that Country, in the Years 1817, 1818, and 1819* [...] (London: John Murray, 1822), p. 336.
93 Latrobe, p. 74; cf. Stanyan, p. 99 on the lack of love between Swiss Catholics and Protestants.
94 Shoberl, p. 158; this would have been Anna Göldin from Glarus, cf. Felicity Rash, 'Metaphors of Darkness and Light in Eveline Hasler's *Anna Göldin, Letzte Hexe* and *Der Riese im Baum*', in *German Contemporary Writers: their Aesthetics and their Language*, ed. by A. Williams, S. Parkes and J. Preece (Bern/Berlin/Frankfurt a.M./New York/Wien: Peter Lang, 1996), pp. 181–200.

Stanhope, on the other hand, writing of the continued practice of torture in many Swiss jurisdictions, condemns what he sees as backward beliefs and practices: 'I might ask whether Switzerland can be considered an enlightened country'.[95]

Conclusion

Many of the visitors to Switzerland documented above followed similar itineraries; they saw the same scenery and monuments, met similar Swiss people, and came away with similar impressions. Some of the most commonly recorded sights, facts and anecdotes are as follows: the armoury in Zürich and the orphanage in Zürich;[96] the fact that the clocks in Basel ran one hour fast;[97] prisoners sweeping the streets of Basel and Bern;[98] the Baths at Baden;[99] sunrise viewed from the Rigi Kulm;[100] stories of the female bandit 'La Belle Batelière' of Brienz (named as Clare Wendell by William Liddiard);[101] goitres and cretins in the Valais;[102] the 'Ranz des Vaches';[103] the paintings of

95   Latrobe, p. 317; Stanhope, p. 81.
96   Thomas Coryat, *Coryat's Crudities* [...], [1611] (reprinted, London: W. Cater, 1776), vol II; Stanhope.
97   Burnet, Martyn.
98   John Moore, *A View of Society and Manners in France, Switzerland and Germany* (London: 1779); Anon, *A Picturesque Tour through France, Switzerland, on the Banks of the Rhine, and through Part of the Netherlands: in the Year MDCCCXVI* (London: printed for J. Mawman, 1817).
99   Coryat, Fynes Moryson, *An Itinerary* [...] *Containing his ten Yeeres Travell through* [...] *the twelve Domjnions of Germany, Bohmerland, Sweitzerland, Netherland, Denmark, Poland, Italy, Turky, France, England, Scotland and Ireland* [...] (London: J. Beale, 1617), William Coxe.
100 Latrobe, Liddiard.
101 Bakewell, Liddiard.
102 Stanyan, William Coxe, Moore, Martyn, Stanhope.
103 William Coxe, op, cit., Byron, Waring, Latrobe, Liddiard.

the 'idiot' Gottfried Mind, the 'Raphael des Chats';[104] the practice of torture to obtain confessions;[105] belief in witches and supernatural forces;[106] the severe sumptuary laws in many cities;[107] yodelling;[108] the 'barbarity' of Swiss German;[109] cowbells;[110] dunghills near human dwellings;[111] the individual freedom and low taxes enjoyed by the Swiss;[112] and the beauty of most Swiss women unless they have goitres (almost all male authors has something to say on one or other aspect of their appearance).

Between the early seventeenth and mid-nineteenth centuries Switzerland was generally praised by British visitors as a place of beauty, liberty and civilisation. A few practices and beliefs were condemned as outdated, such as the belief in witchcraft and the practice of torture, but the Swiss people attracted much acclaim and their way of life, especially their system of government, received many accolades. In 1825 William Hazlitt wrote that he knew of no land more enticing to visitors, where the inhabitants had more grounds for contentment and where 'if you could not find happiness, it seemed in vain to seek farther for it'. For Hazlitt, Switzerland had both extreme wildness and extreme domestic luxury: 'Gigantic sublimity at a distance or over your head, elegance and comfort at your feet'.[113] A mere ten years later Ruskin complained that the British and Swiss together were responsible for disfiguring many of Switzerland's beauty-spots: the former for pleasure and the latter for financial gain. He claimed that the charm of Luzern had been spoiled by the

104 Waring, Stanhope.
105 William Coxe, Stanhope.
106 Addison, Bakewell, Latrobe.
107 Addison, Stanyan, William Coxe.
108 Latrobe, Liddiard.
109 William Coxe, Martyn, Baillie, Liddiard, Agassiz, and both Shelleys.
110 Shoberl, Latrobe
111 Stanhope, Dorothy Wordsworth.
112 Stanyan, Shoberl, William Coxe, Stanhope.
113 Howe, vol 10, p. 294.

erection of a 'large new hotel for the English', which artists should ignore, drawing the houses behind it 'as if it were transparent'; he wrote that the Alps were seen as 'soaped poles in a bear-garden' to be climbed and slid down again 'with shrieks of delight'.[114] Tourism was, however, to become a major industry for Switzerland. As in previous centuries, tourism is seen as having both good and bad aspects: on the one hand it brings prosperity to the country and on the other it is considered by some critics to be the cause of overdevelopment and environmental damage. Foreign visitors are still seen as importing both positive and negative aspects of their own cultures, yet many of the sights, characteristics and traditions described in this essay remain intact.

114 Cook, p. 32; swissinfo, *Early climbers banish dragons* <http://www.swiss-info.org/sen/ swissinfo.html?siteSect=108&sid=751579>, p. 3.

Sue Wilson

An Early Nineteenth-century
English Swiss Cottage at Endsleigh in Devon

Positioning the Study

John Ruskin, using the *nom de plume* Kata Phusin, published *The Poetry of Architecture* in J. C. Loudon's *Architectural Magazine* between 1837 and 1838 and offered in it a notable Victorian eulogy to the Swiss mountain hut in the context of its Alpine setting, but about its imitation on English soil he could not have been more vitriolic.[1] His criticism was aimed at the professionalism of the architect and it was notable that popular designs for Swiss cottages in English architectural *Pattern Books* were withdrawn after Ruskin's publications.[2] However, clients continued to demand a Swiss motif in English cottage architecture throughout the nineteenth century. This is supported by the many examples built after 1838: for instance, at Osborne on the Isle of Wight in 1854 and 1862 for Queen Victoria and Prince Albert, Shrublands Park in Suffolk, Singleton Park in Glamorgan, Spa Chalet at Scarborough in 1860, Rochester Swiss Cottage in Kent for Charles Dickens in 1865, Aston Clinton in Buckinghamshire in 1887 and Teddington Boat House at Richmond about 1888.

1   John Ruskin, *The Poetry of Architecture* (London: George Allen, 1893), p. 46; Ruskin argued that English 'Swiss' cottages were 'incongruous' in the English landscape and therefore only a 'toy', which was 'contemptible'.

2   Peter Frederick Robinson, *Rural Architecture or A Series of Designs for Ornamental Cottages* (London: Rodwell and Martin); Robinson's *Pattern Book* included a *Swiss Cottage* and *a Swiss Farmhouse* and ran to four editions between 1823 and 1836 yet, abruptly in 1838 they were withdrawn.

Architects engaged on English aristocratic country house estates had designed the first wave of built Swiss cottages in England, beginning about 1814. Later, blueprints for a Swiss motif appeared in architectural *Pattern Books* promoting the reinvention of the English country cottage in the context of landscape picturesque and were aimed at English gentlemen with landed estates and arguably pointed to the European 'Grand Tour'. The inclusion of Swiss motifs in architectural *Pattern Books* was ostensibly speculative but evidence suggests that the designers were responding to a market demand. Aesthetically, the English 'Swiss' designs in the *Pattern Books* show a clearer adherence to the indigenous detailing of the Swiss mountain chalet, such as stones to weigh down the roof and Swiss ornamental carving to the elevation, which had not been evident in the early examples on noble estates such as at Cassiobury Park, in Hertfordshire.[3]

This study focuses on one of the earliest bespoke English Swiss cottages at Endsleigh in Devon, built for the sixth Duke and Duchess of Bedford about 1814, ostensibly by the architect Jeffry Wyatt (1766–1840) and within the pleasure grounds designed by Humphry Repton (1752–1818), a renowned landscape gardener of the period.[4] (Figure 1.)

3   A Pattern Book designer, Peter Frederick Robinson, had studied the indigenous Swiss chalet in 1816 en route from Italy; he understood Swiss vernacular architecture to be 'built of timber, on a foundation of stone, and fancifully ornamented by colour, the general face of the building being left without any painting. The Roofs frequently project six and even eight feet, supported by ornamental brackets; they are covered with oak shingles, and are usually loaded with fragments of rock, to prevent the wind from lifting the roof, which might otherwise be the case, in consequence of this great projection. The external stair, or ladder, and the small galleries close under the eves of the roof, give a particular air, or character, to these Cottages', Robinson, p. 29.

4   This investigation is part of a PhD project, *The Nineteenth-century English Swiss Cottage*, and will try to situate the Endsleigh Swiss Cottage within the development of the larger picture as a whole.

Figure 1. Endsleigh Swiss Cottage, front elevation with nineteenth-century steps. Photo: author. By hind permission of The Landmark Trust.

Figure 2. Val d'Anniviers – *village alpestre*. Postcard.

The Lure of the Swiss Alps for the English

From the beginning of the eighteenth century Switzerland was being steadily mapped on the itinerary of the English Grand Tour. The Swiss Alps were objects to conquer, study, write about, paint and be inspired by (Figure 2). To the intrepid Anglo-Saxon, the Swiss mountain chalet was a characteristic feature of the Alpine picturesque, suggesting a Utopian way of life at one with nature's elements and far removed from the complexity of contemporary English culture. *Die Alpen*, written in 1732 by the Swiss Albrecht von Haller (1708–1777), did much to enhance this European view. It contrasted the simple and idyllic way of life in the Alps with the corrupt and decadent existence of the dwellers in the plains.[5]

Generally speaking, the notion of the Swiss picturesque was transmitted in sophisticated English circles through English and European literature, botany, fine art and personal accounts. The best-known figures are continually referred to in literary and art history studies.[6] What appears to be unexplored is how the real experience of the Swiss Alps impacted on the theories and ideas of the picturesque, the sublime and the beautiful.[7] For instance, the seeds of these studies germinated in English romantic poetry, prose and paintings of Switzerland, and in the practice of English landscape architecture and gardens from the middle of the eighteenth century.

5   Albrecht von Haller, *Die Alpen* (1732); the mountains had hitherto been generally regarded as horrible monstrosities in the West.

6   The list is long but the most known are: William Wordsworth (1770–1780), Joseph Mallord William Turner (1775–1851), Lord Byron (1788–1824), Percy Shelley (1792–1824), Mary Shelley (1797–1851), Albert Smith (1816–1860).

7   For example, Horace Walpole in Switzerland 1739, Christian Cay Lorenz Hirschfeld in Switzerland from 1765–1767, 1783; Richard Payne Knight in Switzerland 1776–1779; Sir John Soane in Switzerland 1778, John Ruskin in Switzerland for many years between 1833–1888, Augustus Welby Pugin in Switzerland 1845, 1847.

It is not widely known that the English philosopher Joseph Addison (1672–1719) was a visitor to Switzerland in 1702,. prior to his published writings on the Picturesque. In a letter to William Congreve he wrote of the pleasure evoked by the sublimity of the mountains thirty years before von Haller's poem, which has been characterised as one of the earliest signs of an awakening Western appreciation of mountains. Addison wrote: 'I write to you from the top of the highest mountain in Switzerland… I am here entertained with the prettiest variety of snow-prospects that you can imagine'.[8] The idea of taking pleasure in exploring the darker elements of nature such as the vast woods of an Alpine forest was anticipated for the seventeenth-century Western mind by the third Earl of Shaftsbury (1617–1713) in his popular text *Characteristicks of Men, Manners, Opinions, Times* (1711) which ran to eleven editions.[9] The spectacle of a mountainous landscape incited extreme emotions, and a great garden was in essence expected to evoke a similar, if less powerful, response. At Endsleigh, the ingredients of the landscape as a whole delight and the Swiss cottage is a constituent element

It was William Gilpin (1724–1804) who understood how the imagination contributed to the pleasure of looking at an object in the context of its environment (in this case the Endsleigh Swiss cottage in the context of its natural and built landscape) and how we could be kept entertained by applying the 'mind in examining the beautiful scenes we have found. Sometimes we examine them under the idea

8   W. Graham (ed.), *Letters of Joseph Addison* (Oxford: 1941), in Gavin Rylands de Beer, *Travellers in Switzerland* (London/New York: OUP, 1949).

9   *Characteristicks* is viewed as Shaftsbury's bestseller throughout the eighteenth century; for an enlightened discussion of Shaftsbury, see Tim Mowl, 'Directions from the Grave: The Problem with Lord Shaftsbury', in *Garden History. The Journal of Garden History Society*, no. 1, Spring, 32 (2004), 35–48; I am indebted to Dr. Mowl for recently drawing my attention to Shaftsbury.

of a whole: we admire the composition, the colouring, and the light, in one *comprehensive view*.[10]

Contemporary Accounts and Country House Guides

One of the earliest accounts of the Endsleigh estate was published in 1818.[11] It offered reading for those interested in the private life of the sixth Duke and Duchess of Bedford (John, the sixth Duke being the heir to the estate from 1802) behind their public face at Woburn Abbey, the family seat. The Duke's exuberant Scottish wife, Georgina, who was a constant source of fascination in public life and fashioned trends which others avidly followed, made up for his rather reserved nature.[12]

The vogue for recording important seats of the nobility in England and other parts of the United Kingdom generated a wealth of published literature which proffered descriptions, animated with illustrations and engravings, tempting the aristocracy and sub-aristocracy to take to their carriages and ogle each others' country piles. The Duke's estate at Endsleigh attracted such interest, for although the size of the main house (a *Cottage Orné*) was very modest compared to that of houses built by gentlemen of note, it offered something different, a total work-of-art in the context of the picturesque understood by the *cognoscenti*.

Christopher Hussey has described how the fashion for the *Cottage Orné* originally stemmed from the seduction of 'the simple life', devoid of 'the artificiality of manners and elaboration of gardens at the

---

10 William Gilpin, *Three Essays on Picturesque Beauty*, 2nd ed. (1794), Essay II 'On Picturesque Travel'.

11 J. P. Neale, *Views of the Seats of Noble Gentlemen in England, Wales, Scotland and Ireland* (1818).

12 For an insight into the lives of the sixth Duke and Duchess of Bedford, see Rachel Trethewey, *Mistress of the Arts* (London: Headline, 2002).

beginning of the eighteenth century'.[13] The idea of the cottage dwelling became a fashionable commodity with the English aristocracy, imitating the example of the *chaumière* or *hameau* found on French noble and royal estates. The sixth Duke of Bedford had made people aware of this concept and was already experimenting with a model farm at Woburn Abbey.

The Gentleman's Magazine[14] and Britton's illustrated text on Devonshire,[15] amongst others, published short accounts of the Bedford Westcountry Estate at Endsleigh, which helped to raise its profile. Guides to English country houses, however, were a popular form of literature from the mid-eighteenth century, written in order to inform those who visited country estates.[16] Private estates were open to the public at their owners' discretion, as is still the case today, and now a large number in England are held in trust for the people, with The National Trust and English Heritage being the best-known conservation bodies.

Why were the English nobility and gentry interested in living in the country when the notion of modernity indicated a shift from agrarian living to cultured urbanity? In France, the focus was on the French court in Paris and Versailles which led to a development of the French town house. In England, the concentration was on its political leaders where their mansions and parks were in the countryside. Their estates were seen as creative hubs of social, literary and artistic culture to be studied and imitated, with their houses and landscape architecture refashioned at great expense in the latest styles.

13   Christopher Hussey, 'Endsleigh Devon – II', in *Country Life*, 10 August 1961.

14   *The Gentleman's Magazine*, 1830, pp. 220–21.

15   John Britton and E.W. Brayley, *Devonshire Illustrated* (1832); Britton was a respected networker and producer of lavish texts on noble seats.

16   See John Harris, 'English Country House Guide', in John Summerson (ed.), *Concerning architecture: essays on architectural writers and writing* (London: Lane, 1968).

Arguably, the English politicians and aristocrats had notable houses in London, too, but the real focus was on their country house estates. The sixth Duke of Bedford lavishly embellished Woburn Abbey, employing contemporary English architects and landscape designers. The Abbey was seen as an exemplary seat commanding one of the highest profiles in English polite society. So why the popular fascination with the Duke's minor estate in Devon?

Topography and the Historical Development of the Endsleigh Estate

The Endsleigh Estate lies in an isolated valley between the village of Tavistock in the east, Launceston in the west, and Plymouth in the south. The Tamar River carves its way through it, demarcating the county boundary of Devon and Cornwall. In the medieval period during the reign of Richard II, Endsleigh was attached to the Abbey at Tavistock and used as a park, after the abbots had acquired it from the Edgcumbe family of Cotehele in Cornwall. With the dissolution of the monasteries, Henry VIII gave the Tavistock Estate to Lord Russell, the Earl of Bedford, for services rendered to the country. William Russell, the fifth descendant, acquired the titles of Marquis of Tavistock and the Duke of Bedford during the reign of William and Mary.

The Tamar valley offered a central location to the sixth Duke of Bedford's principal estates in the south-west, his possessions in the north of Devon, and those in the county of Cornwall. It produced considerable revenue from the mineral resources mined on the estate, for which the Duke was interested in overseeing improvements, and it offered a family seat for his title, the Marquis of Tavistock. A stone plaque on the estate states that the Duchess of Bedford chose Endsleigh as the 'spot' for a family retreat, having identified its 'natural' and 'picturesque beauties' suitable for the project.[17] Georgina, the Duchess of Bedford (née Gordon) was familiar with cottage architecture as a rural retreat. As a child, she regularly took family holidays away from the formality of polite society at Gordon Castle in Moray, Scotland, at their rural lodge, Glenfiddich, in a wooded, mountainous and secluded valley. The Duchess of Gordon immersed her children in a bucolic lifestyle at Glenfiddich, engaging them directly with nature, a stark contrast to the artificiality of social etiquette demanded of an aristocratic lifestyle.[18] Therefore, the idea of building a rural retreat on the historic and picturesque estate at Tavistock, away from the public gaze at Woburn Abbey, was arguably something the Duchess would favour, a chance to nurture her own children in nature's elements.

Endsleigh can be described as 'picturesque' even to the twenty-first century global traveller: the house, cottages, paths, gardens and grounds fuse with the valley's natural elements, projecting a pleasing effect. To the nineteenth-century visitor, it stirred stronger emotions but then, in general, people had not travelled very far to experience variety and make comparisons. When an English landscape was described as 'wild and picturesque' it conjured up a very different picture in the mind for those who had traversed the Swiss Alps. However, in principle the underlying characteristics, which formed a scenic view described as picturesque, were arguably similar. In the

17   The Plaque is in the stable courtyard at Endsleigh and reads: 'Endsleigh cottage was built as a residence in this sequestered valley by John, Duke of Bedford, the spot having been preciously chosen for the natural and picturesque beauties which surround it by Georgiana, Duchess of Bedford. Her four eldest sons laid the first stone of the building [...] September 7, 1810'.

18   A model farm was built for the children to engage them with animals and encourage them to open their senses to the pleasures of nature. A goat provided the children with fresh milk for its medicinal properties against illness; Georgina Bedford (sixth Duchess) followed her mother's lead taking a cow with her on continental tours to supply her children with fresh milk.

Swiss Alps, the sublimity of the mountains did not appear terrifying alongside the rustic vocabulary of Alpine life such as mountain huts, shepherds and cows. The scene then appeared picturesque, not terrifying or 'horrid'. In such a context, the Western fear of the mountains was arguably overcome. In rural England, a rugged landscape which contained picturesque elements, such as rocks, undulating terrain and rapidly running water, appeared 'wild' yet with the introduction of an appropriate building and garden into the landscape, it became 'picturesque'. This was how Humphry Repton understood his assignment for the landscaping and cultivation of the Endsleigh garden and pleasure grounds: 'Without the aid of art, the most romantic or picturesque scenery in nature is a desert, and only fitted to the habitation of wild beasts'.[19]

Jeffry Wyatt and Humphry Repton inherited built elements at Endsleigh, which, together with its natural features, influenced the design of the grounds and architecture. The site on which Wyatt was eventually commissioned to design and build the main house already had an existing building on it. This was a simple, irregular farmhouse poised in the lee of a wooded hillside fronting the River Tamar. The farmhouse and its setting presented a picturesque composition which had captured the Duke's imagination. It was Repton and not Wyatt who presented the initial plan and elevation for the Duke's main house at Endsleigh in 1809. These reflected the hand of Repton's son George, who had been apprenticed to John Nash and was well versed in the style of the *Cottage Orné*. The Repton design presented a conglomeration of thatched cottages, seemingly inspired by the existing house which the Duke had already expressed a desire to retain.

> *The irregular farm-house* presented an object that was so picturesque, that it was impossible to wish it removed and replaced by any other style of building that architecture had hitherto invented, viz, a castle,

19　Repton, *The Cottage* (1816), p. 593.

or an abbey, or a palace, not one of which could be so applicable to the scenery as this cottage, or rather, group of rural buildings.[20]

The existing farmhouse was in fact removed and replaced by a more 'lavish' style of cottage by Jeffry Wyatt in 1810:[21]

> *Jeffry Wyatt's Cottage Orné* looked a little raw to Repton when he was brought in later to landscape the grounds, but he appreciated the way its horseshoe shape exploited the picturesque possibilities of the great meander of the Tamar, with apartments angled to various views up and down the river, Wyatville's design has distinctly Reptonian features.[22]

There is a faint touch of irony in the Duke's patronage of Jeffry Wyatt and Humphry Repton. Wyatt replaced Repton in the design and building of the architectural features at Endsleigh in 1810 and Repton replaced Wyatt in the landscaping of its grounds in 1814.

Wyatt could turn his hand to any number of architectural styles, a necessary prerequisite for the demands of his informed patrons. Wyatt's early commissions fashioned a degree of irregularity in country houses and villas, which at Endsleigh was clearly pronounced. His principal essay on the Endsleigh *Cottage Orné* embraced the fashion for cottage architecture on country estates, moulded the plan to the shape of the land and introduced materials sympathetic to its topography. Jeffry Wyatt's work echoed, in practice, what was theoretically being promoted in academic circles, namely, to 'accommodate his building to the scenery, not make that give way

---

20 ibid, pp. 213–26.
21 Stephen Daniels, *Humphry Repton: Landscape Gardening and the Geography of Georgian England* (New Haven/London: Yale University Press, 1999), p. 185.
22 ibid, p. 186; Daniels refers to the architect of the *Cottage Orné* as (Jeffry) Wyatville when in fact in 1810 he was still known as (Jeffry) Wyatt; he had commenced the Endsleigh *Cottage Orné* in 1810 under his birth name of Wyatt, but it was not until 1824 that he changed his name to Wyatville.

to the building'.[23] Given the Duke of Bedford's sensitivity to the existing built features on the estate, it is debatable whether the architect or the patron had the upper hand in the style and feel for the new project. What is clearly expressed from the complete ensemble at Endsleigh is that the approach to all aspects of its composition showed a synthesis of contemporary thinking, practice and fashion of its day. Both Jeffry Wyatt's and Humphry Repton's principal work on the estate have been documented. For a fuller account the reader is directed to those authorities that have published on the subject.[24]

It could be argued that the *Cottage Orné* (the style in which Wyatt's principal elevation at Endsleigh is built)[25] was the forerunner of the introduction of the English 'Swiss' cottage. However, the Endsleigh example of a *Cottage Orné* shows no immediate aesthetic similarity to the Endsleigh Swiss cottage. The same problem is encountered when we compare an indigenous Swiss chalet and its Endsleigh hybrid. The enquiry has to be philosophically explored to determine the correlation. In principle, the question of similarity and difference can be discussed in relation to characteristic features and contexts (natural topography, social culture, theoretical agendas of the picturesque and fashion). For example, to make a comparative study between the *Cottage Orné* at Endsleigh by Jeffry Wyatt around 1814, and the *Cottage Orné* (called Swiss Cottage) at Cahir, Country Tipperary, Ireland by John Nash (1752–1835) around 1812, it would be necessary to discuss characteristic features and contexts in order to assert that they are indeed the same type of building, since this

---

23 Uvedale Price, *Essays on the Picturesque* (1798), p. 360ff in <www. oxforddnb.com>, by D. Linstrum (Oxford University Press, 2004).

24 Derek Linstrum, *Sir Jeffry Wyatville: Architect to the King* (Oxford: Clarendon Press, 1972), pp. 88–97; Christopher Hussey, 'Endsleigh, Devon – I & II', in *Country Life*, August 1961, p. 246ff, p. 296ff; John Cornforth, 'Endsleigh House, Devon – I'. in *Country Life*, 9 October 1997, pp. 58–62, 16 October 1997, pp. 62–5.

25 Hussey (1961), p. 246f., p. 296f.

is not immediately apparent from the profile of their elevations.[26] Arguably, the same approaches need to be undertaken to determine the 'Swissness' of an English Swiss cottage. (Figure 3 and 4.)

John Nash had established a rustic cottage style, prior to any work by Jeffry Wyatt, in response to the vogue for a rustic simplicity but it is not clear who took the lead in integrating a 'Swiss' character into their elevations. Notably, Repton worked simultaneously with both architects, on various country house commissions, incorporating designs for cottages to ornament his landscape plans. Often his sons, John Adey and George Repton were called on to research and produce the designs for buildings which complemented their father's landscaped proposals.

The surge of interest in English cottages by the gentleman landowner was reflected in the English architectural *Pattern Books*, which arguably promoted the idea of a bucolic simplicity as a desirable rural built aesthetic to a wider audience. Early authors included Plaw (1794, 1795 and 1800), Lugar (1805, 1807), Gandy (1805) and Gyfford (1807). Notably, Plaw was engaged by the fifth Duke of Gordon, producing designs for his 'hunting lodge' at Glenfiddich in Scotland, which provided more elements for the Endsleigh project.

The introduction of a 'Swiss' motif appeared in the cottage *Pattern Books* from approximately 1818 (Papworth), though devoid of any reference to the Endsleigh or Cahir examples already mentioned. A clearly expressed set of guidelines for the Swiss chalet style was promoted to a popular audience by Peter Frederick Robinson (1776–1858), an architect who excited the minds of millions with a Swiss Alpine exhibit that included a 'faux Swiss chalet' and mountain grotto at The Colosseum in Regent's Park, London from 1829–1851 and whose architectural *Pattern Books* delivered quality blue-prints of

---

26   The Cahir example of a *Cottage Orné*, attributed to John Nash, is known as Swiss Cottage, and was built for Richard Lord Cahir in 1812; this has to be considered as an important forerunner of the English development of Swiss Cottages given the reference to its Swissness.

Figure 3. General view of the south and east fronts of the *Cottage Orné* by Jeffry Wyatt at Endsleigh, from Humphry Burton's *Red Book of Endsleigh* (1814) in the collection in Woburn Abbey, Bedfordshire. By kind permission of His Grace the Duke of Bedford and the Trustees of the Bedford Estates.

Figure 4. The *Cottage Orné* at Cahir, County Tipperary, Ireland by John Nash circa 1812, called *Swiss Cottage*. Photo: Department of the Environment, Heritage and Local Government.

the Swiss cottage style for a popular audience which went to many editions. The later publications generating Swiss cottages were by Loudon (1832) and Goodwin (1834).

The Endsleigh Swiss Cottage

The nineteenth century Endsleigh Swiss cottage is the earliest example of its type listed in the English National Monument Records which remains in its original form and location. It was built for the sixth Duke and Duchess of Bedford and remained in the ownership of the family up until the middle of the twentieth century. It remained disused for many years and fell into a state of disrepair. A decision was made to sell it in 1977 to The Landmark Trust for restoration and conservation and in 1978 it became a Grade I listed building.

The Endsleigh Swiss Cottage is an important example in the chronology of nineteenth-century English Swiss cottages and the first known example in England. It does not correlate to any of the 'Swiss style' designs published in *Pattern Books* at the beginning of the nineteenth century or refer to any previously built motif in England. Furthermore, neither its owners nor attributed architects have left evidence of their motive or sources for building it as it is and thus contexts play an important part of its study. The Swiss Cottage has been referred to in reviews of the estate as background detail to Wyatt's main essay and Repton's landscaping,[27] and as a listed building there is a description of its current construction; further than this, little has been published.

Location

Geographically, the Swiss Cottage lies 720 metres to the south-east of the main house, beyond the garden and pleasure gardens groomed by

---

27 Hussey (1961), Cornforth (1997); there is a nineteenth-century reference: John Britton and E.W. Broughley, *Devonshire Illustrated* (1832).

Repton, tracing the natural curvature of the ground to the Shell House and Grotto, into the pleasure grounds heading out on a network of walks and drives which extend south-east and south into Leigh Wood. The Swiss Cottage stands on high ground with panoramic views to the main house and across the Tamar valley towards the distant hills of Cornwall. (Figure 5.) A written description by Repton of the estate gives a sense of the view of the valley towards the hills, which one experiences from the Swiss Cottage: 'Here, Solitude, embosomed in all the sublimity of umbrageous majesty, looks down on the infant river, struggling through its rocky channel, and hurtling onwards with all the impetuosity of ungoverned youth'.[28]

The Swiss Cottage was the destination for an ascending walk in the pleasure grounds on the estate, reached by a 'zigzagged' climb to an Alpine garden, which surrounded the Cottage. The date and authorship of the Alpine garden is problematic in that Repton makes no allusion to it in his 'Red Book' which he kept as the landscape gardener of the gardens and pleasure grounds at Endsleigh. The Alpine garden no longer exists though an unknown artist captured in watercolour an idea of how it looked.[29] The surrounding land to the Swiss Cottage is simply laid to a grass terrace where early nine-teenth-century stone steps descend to the lower walks by the river, west of the cottage.

Determining Date and Authenticity

Twentieth-century descriptions date the Swiss Cottage as having been built around 1810, the date Jeffry Wyatt was given the commission to design and build the main residence at Endsleigh. John Britton was the first to record the presence of the Swiss Cottage on the Bedford seat in 1832.[30] Neale had not alluded to it in his commentary

28 Repton, *Situation and Character* (1816), p. 587.
29 Two unsigned watercolours of the Endsleigh Swiss Cottage are held at Woburn Abbey, possibly from the 1820s and 1830s, reference: misc. 1041, 1021.
30 J. Britton and E.W. Broughley, pp. 55–6.

Figure 5. Perspective from Endsleigh Swiss Cottage towards the *Cottage Orné* (now Endsleigh Hotel). Photo: author. By kind permission of The Landmark Trust.

of 1818 which suggests that Neale had either considered the Swiss Cottage not worthy of note, or possibly that it had yet to be built.[31] Moreover, had the Swiss motif been realised by Wyatt around 1814, Repton would have referred to it in his proposals for the landscaping of the Endsleigh grounds and garden; furthermore, had the Swiss Cottage been in Repton's hand, it would have materialised in his 'Red Book'. Therefore can we assume that Humphry Repton was not the designer of the Swiss Cottage or that Jeffry Wyatt had yet to design or build it before 1814?

However, there is a point which needs to be explored before Repton can be dismissed as the author of the Endsleigh Swiss Cottage. Repton's drawings for the landscaping at Endsleigh indicated a building south-southeast of the main house in Leigh Wood. This building appears in Repton's plans for Endsleigh in his 'Red Book' of 1814 but there is no written reference to it in the text. It takes the form in the plan of a one-storey, white Grecian temple, with a pyramidal roof supported by four columns, resting on the lower bank of the River Tamar and further along the river-bed from the Swiss Cottage. Repton does not explain what this building is. Furthermore, there are two other known built structures on the same side of the river-bank to the Swiss Cottage which have not been listed in English National Monument Records. The first is a boathouse, which still exists, though it is not known who built this and when, and the second is the 'Rustic Seat for Warm Wood' designed by Jeffry Wyatt, identified by Linstrum from a drawing around 1820.

Derek Linstrum, Jeffry Wyatt's biographer and cataloguer of works, identifies Sir Jeffry Wyatville as the architect for the Endsleigh

---

31 The sixth Duke of Bedford's correspondence has not been catalogued though is currently being evaluated by a biographer; to date references to Endsleigh, Wyatville and Switzerland have not been found; the Duke's heir, as a result of a rift in their relationship, has possibly destroyed accounts by the Duchess of Bedford; estate accounts have yet to be searched at Devon Record Office.

32 Linstrum, *Sir Jeffry Wyattville*, p. 95.

Swiss Cottage but does not discuss the problematic issue of date.[32] It is evident from Linstrum's catalogue that Wyatt continued to work on the Endsleigh estate after 1810 with two drawings for minor buildings dated 1814 and 1816[33] and an 1820 design for 'A Rustic Seat for Warm Wood'. As the bulk of the architectural drawings for the estate are missing from the Endsleigh volume of Wyatville's work,[34] it remains difficult to assess accurately when the Swiss Cottage was built at Endsleigh. The only current evidence known to the author is that Sir Jeffry Wyatville painted the Endsleigh Swiss Cottage elevation after 1828.[35]

External, Formal Description

The Swiss Cottage is listed as an early nineteenth century, three-storeyed, timber-framed structure, clad with rustic planking and a thatched roof, gabled on the second floor to the front, which hangs over a three-sided balcony. An external wooden staircase at the side leads to the first floor balcony with access to the upper rooms from a half-glazed door in the centre of the front elevation. The balcony is carried from the ground floor by notched wooden posts and timber struts (two additional wooden posts have since been added to the front elevation). All facades are faced with split logs, their bark attached

33 The 1814 drawing for a Dairy (not found in Linstrum's catalogue of Wyatville's works but suggested in Linstrum's biography of Wyatville), and an 1816 drawing for a Sun Dial, as attributed in D. Linstrum, *Catalogue of the Drawings Collection of the Royal Institute of British Architects: The Wyatt Family* (Farnborough: Gregg International Publishers, 1973), p. 60.

34 Linstrum accounts for the missing drawings from a hand-written note by Wyatville in the volume of drawings; Wyatt notes that these were removed for copying in 1835 for the sixth Duke of Bedford so that he could send these to 'Prince Esterhazy of Hungary'.

35 It is possible that further documentation in the Bedford Papers held at the Devon Record Office could provide evidence on the local tradesmen and suppliers engaged to erect the Swiss Cottage; this has yet to be determined.

and fixed horizontally, vertically and diagonally to the timber frame. A timber pinnacle is attached to a wooden pendant on the front and side gable of the house although Wyatville did not include them in his watercolour of the elevation.[36] The building stands alone, perched on a grass terrace, yet it remains hidden against its wooded backdrop.

Interior

Britton's 1832 account of the Swiss Cottage at Endsleigh has been regularly drawn on as a contemporary source for a general account of the estate, but it also contains a reference to its use and to some of the objects inside. This in itself implies that the inclusion of the Swiss Cottage in the grounds of the Endsleigh estate was not perceived simply as an *objet d'art* for the landscape but that it was intended for use. The three floors had a specific demarcation and purpose. The lower ground floor rooms and upper second were solely for its housekeeper/estate labourer, and the second floor (accessed from the external and internal staircase) was for the Bedfords and their guests. Britton describes the contents of the upper apartments as being furnished "'à la Suisse" with wooden chairs and platters, hornspoons, etc. for the occasional visits of the Bedford family'.[37] Contemporary references to Swiss furnishings and fittings in English Swiss cottages are fairly rare, but Endsleigh is not an isolated example. The Royal Swiss Cottages at Osborne, Isle of Wight were furnished with ornate and functional objects bought either in Switzerland, at the Great Exhibition of 1851 or copied from Swiss sources.

It is not known how the Bedford family have used the Swiss Cottage over the last two centuries, but it would be a fair assumption that it was occupied up until its sale in 1953 in much the same manner as Britton observed in 1832. The Bedfords used their West-

36 Two nineteenth-century watercolours of the Endsleigh Swiss Cottage, belonging to His Grace the 15th Duke of Bedford, clearly show both pinnacles, reference: Woburn Abbey, misc 1041 and misc 102.

37 Britton, p. 56.

Figure 6. Endsleigh Swiss Cottage elevation by Sir Jeffry Wyatville (n.d.) Watercolour. Courtesy of the R.I.B.A. Photographics Collection.

country seat as an occasional retreat from the formality of Woburn. When they visited, they brought a full complement of staff so as not to compromise their comfortable lifestyle. Although Endsleigh was considered the private domain of the Bedfords, they opened it to invited guests when it was not in use by the family. Lord and Lady Grey were visitors in 1824 and this had not been their first visit.[38]

Design Influences and Possible Sources

The Endsleigh Swiss Cottage shows distinct similarities to the one (since demolished) at Cassiobury Park, Hertfordshire where Jeffry Wyatt is known to have been working in 1817. It has been assumed that the Endsleigh Swiss Cottage was built before the Cassiobury model but this is not certain. Britton's album, published in 1837, of the seat of the Earl of Essex at Cassiobury claims that Wyatt was responsible for the Cassiobury Swiss Cottage and some of the *Cottages Ornés* in the park, although dates for their construction are unclear.[39] (Figures 6 and 7) The Endsleigh Swiss Cottage may have been the model for other Swiss buildings at Claverton Manor, Bath around 1820 and Langold Park Estate, Yorkshire around 1817, where Wyatt was working at the time when he was engaged at Endsleigh. Others at Bulstrode Park, around 1812 and Virginia Water, Windsor, between about 1824 and 1828, need further investigation. There is a fundamental point regarding Jeffry Wyatt as the architect of English Swiss cottages: there is no evidence to suggest that he studied the Swiss chalet pattern in Switzerland. Linstrum makes no mention of Wyatt travelling to Switzerland. Therefore, if he was commissioned to design Swiss cottages for English clients what was his source of reference? One suggestion could be that he cobbled together elements found in illustrated texts either from his own collection of books or from collections held by others. In the 1790s, Jeffry

38 Grey Papers, University of Durham: GRE/B6/16/13 (27.09.1823), GRE/B6/17/83–83a (14/15.01.1824), GRE/B6/17/85 (12.04.1824), GRE/B6/16/13a (12.09.1824), GRE/B6/16/14 (20.09.1824).

39 Linstrum, *Sir Jeffry Wyattville*, p. 234.

Figure 7. Elevation and plan of Cassiobury Swiss Cottage by A.C. Pugin, from John Britton, *The History and Description, with Graphic Illustration, of Cassiobury Park, Hertfordshire* (1837), plates xv, xvi. By kind permission of the British Library.

Wyatt had access to the extensive library at Fonthill Abbey during his apprenticeship to his uncle, James Wyatt (1746–1813), who was then engaged at Fonthill by William Beckford (1760–1844), an eminent collector of fine art books. Beckford was a frequent visitor to Switzerland between 1777 and 1802 and was well connected with Swiss *literati* and scientists. His earliest visit to Switzerland was part of a Grand Tour in 1780 during which he had with him the *Idylls* of the Swiss artist and writer Salomon Gessner[40] which filled the young tourist's mind with ideas of Arcadian pleasures. For Beckford, Switzerland presented the reality of Gessner's idealisations of pastoral life.[41] The library at Fonthill contained twenty thousand books collected by Beckford, many of which related to Switzerland. Works that he owned included *The Idylliums of Theocritus* in Fawkes' 1767 translation, as well as Gessner (*Oeuvres*) *Idyilles, & Entableaus Dessinés par Berbier*, and *Rousseau (Oeuvres de Jean Jaques)*, 1769. These volumes had been a turning point for Beckford, bringing about his 'overriding emotional appreciation of the landscape, which he coveted as a consoling alternative to the dullness to society'.[42] Additionally, C. C. Hirshfeld, *Théorie des Jardins, ou L'Art des Jardins de la Nature*, (1802)[43] had been important in the development of garden art with references to the Swiss picturesque. Switzerland had a profound effect on Beckford, he became caught up with the English pursuit of the sublime in the Swiss Alps: 'Hours of wonder and gratitude. I have been steeped in those sensations which arise from

40 Idylls were rococo versions of Theocritan Ecloques, widely translated and enjoyed in English from 1762, see Tim Mowl, *William Beckford Composing for Mozart* (London: Murray, 1998), pp. 54–81.

41 Beckford delighted in charades of pastoral life; Gessner's *New Idylles* (1776) was avidly consumed by the British with one or more of the separate *Idylles* appearing in seventeen different periodicals in one year alone. Mowl, *William Beckford*, p. 81.

42 Mowl, *William Beckford*, p. 65.

43 *The Valuable Library of Books in Fonthill Abbey*, A Catalogue for Auction, 9 September–31 October 1823.

the contemplation of the great objects of nature'.[44] His regeneration of a disused quarry at Fonthill into an Alpine garden containing a wooden mountain hut by Joseph Lane in the mid 1790s[45] was testimony to his awakened sense of the Alpine picturesque. It is possible that William Beckford's Alpine garden could have been the model for the Alpine garden at Endsleigh Swiss Cottage if this was Jeffry Wyatt's concern.

There does not appear to be a published pattern for an English Swiss style of cottage before 1818. However, the publications of 1809 and 1810 by Johann Carl Krafft (1764–1833), *Plans of the Most Beautiful Picturesque Gardens in France, England and Germany, and of the edifices, monuments, fabrics, etc., which contribute to their embellishment, of every kind of Architecture, such as Chinese, Egyptian, Arabian, Moorish, etc.*, show elevations for a French-Swiss farm entrance, French-Swiss farm house, French agricultural building for cattle and forage in a French-Swiss style and a French-Swiss dairy[46] by the architect Kléber who had produced them for the Prince of Montbéliard in 1787 as minor buildings for his estate in Alsace. (Figure 8) These books were produced in French with English and German summaries and were aimed internationally at architects and 'lovers of the arts' engaged in the design and construction of country house gardens where built ornament was intrinsic to a picturesque context.

44 Hamilton Papers, Red Copy Book, No.16; From the summit of Mount Salève, 9 o'clock, Sept. 13, 1777, in William Beckford, *The Grand Tour of William Beckford*, ed. by Elizabeth Mavor (Hamondsworth: Penguin, 1986), p.12.

45 The hut is described as 'Norwegian' in contemporary sources, but its effect was that aimed for by the landscape architects with Swiss cottages, namely, to be in 'tasteful proportions' and 'in perfect harmony with the general scenery', Rutter, *Delineations of Fonthill Abbey* (1823), chapter 4, p. 91.

46 J. Krafft, *Des Plus Beaux Jardins Pittoresques De France, D'Angleterre et D'Allemagne* (Paris: Levrault, 1809, 1810), vol I, Plates xxv, xxvi, xxviii, xxix, xxx.

> Since their [gardens'] embellishment consists partly in the erection
> of little allegorical monuments, the whole richness of which depends
> but on their ornaments, these gardens therefore, could not remain any
> longer under the direction of mere ordinary gardeners, but become
> the province of perfection.[47]

Krafft set out to present the best examples of French garden picturesque which profiled unknown French artists. He also included
a selection of English and German gardens that had adopted the
French model. The French-Swiss farm ensemble on the Montbéliard
estate in Alsace ornamented the pleasure grounds alongside other
buildings which included temples, cottages, houses, huts and sundry
garden structures in Gothic, Moresque, Chinese, Tyrolian, Polish and
Turkish styles. Each building had a practical function, many were built
of wood, were embellished and some had a thatched roof.

The idea of a *faux* village, placed in the grounds of an aristocratic
seat and evoking a bucolic lifestyle, was not original to the Montbéliard
seat. Marie Antoinette's *hameau* at Versailles was completed in 1783
with Swiss embellishments and is thought to have been a copy of
another built for the Prince de Condé, amongst others.[48]

The importance of Krafft's publications of 1809 and 1810 is that
he made Kléber's plans of 1787 internationally available as a design
source. Furthermore, the designs show a visual link to Endsleigh Swiss
Cottage and the Cassiobury Park Swiss Cottage in Hertfordshire
thought also to have been designed by Jeffry Wyatt. Kléber's plans
show a design for a three-storey elevation with a three-sided balcony,
accessed by external stairs, a thatched roof with overhangs to the first-
floor galleries and use of vertical, horizontal and diagonal rough-hewn
timber facing, all of which are characteristic of the Endsleigh and
Cassiobury Swiss Cottages. (Figure 9)

47 Krafft, 'Préface'.
48 Antonia Fraser, *Marie Antoinette, Queen, Consort of Louis XVI, King
    of France, 1755–1793* (London: Weidenfeld & Nicholson, 2001), pp.
    245–47.

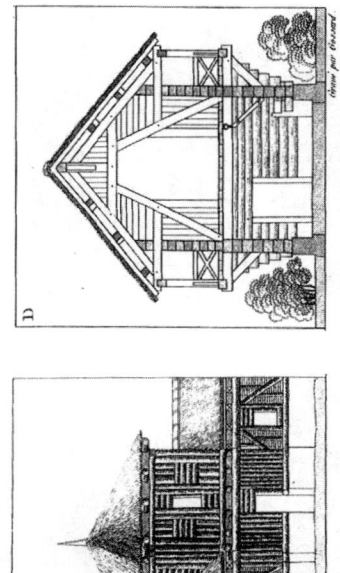

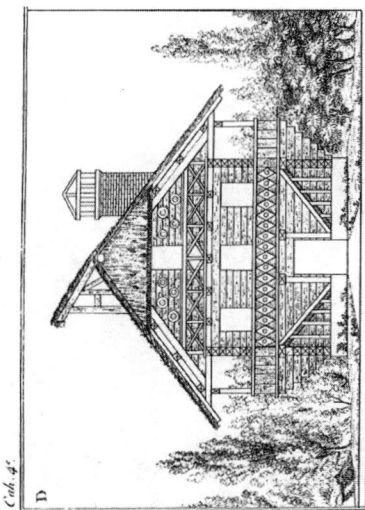

Figure 8. Possible design sources for Endsleigh and Cassiobury Swiss Cottages, French elevations built circa 1787 in Alsace, from John Krafft, *Des Plus Beaux Jardins Pittoresques De France, D'Angleterre et D'Allemagne* (Paris: Levrault, 1809), vol. I, plates xxvi, xxvii, xxviii, xxix (parts of). By kind permission of The british Library.

Figure 9. Endsleigh Swiss Cottage, side elevation; the application of the split-log cladding shows similarity to the elevation published by John Krafft in 1809. Photo: author. By kind permission of The Landmark trust.

Other possible sources for the Swiss characteristics of the Swiss Cottage at Endsleigh were Jeffry Wyatt's clients. The Duke and Duchess of Bedford were well travelled in Europe, completing a two year tour in 1815 after having visited Portugal, Spain, Gibraltar, Italy (Florence, Naples and Rome) and France (Paris) although it is not known if they were in Switzerland.[49] The Duke and Duchess kept abreast of contemporary thinking and were committed to the patronage and promotion of English art and architecture and its fashioned styles, and they promulgated their tastes not only to an English cultural elite but also to an interested public. Their library at Woburn Abbey was extensive and contained descriptions and images of foreign voyages, including important texts on the Swiss Alps.[50] The development of the Duke's model farm at Woburn kept his library shelves stocked with architectural *Pattern Books* on rural architecture and ornamental cottages, which included designs for buildings in a 'Swiss style', some predating Jeffry Wyatt's engagement at Endsleigh.[51] It is highly probable that the Duke had Krafft's 1809 and 1810 books in his library. It is also possible that the Duke and Duchess of Bedford were invited visitors to French noble and aristocratic seats and therefore privy to the model villages which contained references to the Swiss architectural motif.

49 Trethewey, p. 148.
50 The Duke's library contained sub-headings for Switzerland and the Alps and included texts such as H. B. Saussure, *Voyages dans les Alpes*, 2 vols (Neufchâtel: 1779–1786).
51 W. Wright, *Grotesque Architecture* (1802); R. Elsam, *Essay on Rural Architecture* (1805); J. Plaw, *Rural Architecture* (1802); J. Plaw, *Ferme Ornée*, (1805); E. Bartell, *Hints for the improvements in ornamental cottages* (1804); J. Gandy, *Designs for cottages etc.* (1805); J. Gandy, *The Rural Architect* (1805); C. Waistell, *Designs for Agricultural Buildings* (1827); P. F. Robinson, *Rural Architecture* (1828); P. F. Robinson, *Designs for Farm Buildings* (1803); J. C. Loudon, *Encyclopedia Plans and Elevations Designed for Cottages* (1833).

The Duchess of Bedford's family, the Duke and Duchess of Gordon, made several visits in the eighteenth century to Switzerland.[52] They too had a rural summer house at Glenfiddich built to the plans of John Plaw in 1800, a fashionable architect publishing *Pattern Books* for cottage and farm architecture from 1794 'made for, and adapted to particular situations'.[53] In 1834 a Swiss Cottage was built as an entrance gate to the Gordon Castle Estate in Banffshire, Scotland.[54]

The importance of published accounts of Switzerland in England at the end of the eighteenth century cannot be overstated. For example, in 1793 Joseph Johnson published the account by William Wordsworth (1770–1850) of his 1790 walking tour of Switzerland,[55] subsequently reworked for the 1805 edition of *The Prelude*. Here Wordsworth observed the Alpine picturesque embracing the Swiss mountain chalet:

> My heart lept up when first I did look down
> On that which was first seen of those deep haunts,
> A green recess, an aboriginal vale,
> Quiet and lorded over and possessed
> By naked huts, wood-built, and sown like tents
> Or Indian cabins over the fresh lawns
> And by the river side.[56]

52 The fourth Duke of Gordon won an archery competition in Geneva in 1761 and bought farm equipment there in 1764 and 1766, and his son was in Lausanne in 1782. Historically, the third Duke of Gordon had engaged a Swiss valet in the middle of the eighteenth century and the fifth Duke employed a Swiss gamekeeper, <http://www.rcahms.gov.uk>. GD44/52/134.

53 _<www.rcahms.gov.uk>. NMRS NJ33SW 9.

54 The Gordon Castle Swiss Cottage is the only one listed in National Monument Records in Scotland, RCAHMS GD44/53/25/12; it has been compared to a pattern published in Loudon (1833).

55 William Wordsworth, *Descriptive Sketches. In verse. Taken during a Pedestrian Tour in the Italian, Grison, Swiss, and Savoyard Alps* (London: Johnson, 1793).

Georgina Bedford's society contemporary and rival, the Duchess of Devonshire, published an account of Switzerland in 1799, a romantic eulogy of her visit, which first appeared in 1802 and resonating with Wordsworth's description of his passage from France to Switzerland; it was enormously popular and was translated into French and German.

It is probable that the idea for the Swiss cottage at Endsleigh came from the sixth Duke and Duchess of Bedford, the building designed by Jeffry Wyatt with reference to Krafft's plans and elevations of French-Swiss buildings and influenced by William Beckford's Alpine garden at Fonthill Abbey. The Duchess of Bedford saw the Endsleigh Estate as her retreat from her high-society profile at Woburn Abbey and valued Endsleigh's natural beauties above all other Bedford properties: 'Your father and I created it [Endsleigh] together, every walk, every plant and most of the trees, for years we watched their growth – and such another place I do not believe is to be found'.[57]

The Endsleigh estate is now open to the public in various ways: the grounds for public perambulation, the *Cottage Orné* as a boutique hotel, and the Swiss Cottage as an established holiday let owned by The Landmark Trust. The Endsleigh Swiss Cottage, like the Endsleigh *Cottage Orné*, has either been dismissed or attracted criticism, but as a motif in a picturesque composition of the Endsleigh estate it is considered to be one of the best complete examples of Regency Picturesque taste.

---

56 William Wordsworth, *The Prelude*, A Parallel Text, ed. by J.C. Maxwell (London, New Haven: Yale University Press, 1981, c1971), Book VI, 'Cambridge and The Alps' (1805), p. 232 [lines 509–15].

57 Sixth Duchess of Bedford to Lord John Russell (her stepson), 1841, PRO Kew 30/22/4a, in Trethewey, p. 281.

Literature

Tom Hubbard

Austere Intoxications:
Literary Relations between Scotland and
Switzerland from 1782 to the Present

From 1806 to 1808 a young Swiss geologist, Louis Necker de Saussure (1786–1861) visited Scotland, including the Hebrides, and some fourteen years later he published an account of his travels.[1] As a seeker after facts he was not obviously susceptible to poetry and music but he was nevertheless moved by the Gaelic songs of the boatmen of Ulva, while confessing his ignorance of the airs and the words.[2] We smile at someone who takes his pleasures so earnestly.

Necker detected a temperamental affinity between the Swiss and the Scots. On Iona, he found that a people who lived in a foggy, dreary climate could yet possess such a cheerful disposition as we would associate with the nations of southern Europe. How far this might co-exist with the notorious dourness of lowland Scots (and of non-Ticinesi Swiss) is open to question. But if collective psychologies mean anything, together with the cultural qualities which they inform and by which they are informed, we may be able to detect a web of relationships that is more subtle and complex than stereotypes would allow. Scotland and Switzerland are each large enough to contain contradictions.

1   Louis Necker de Saussure, *Voyages en Ecosse et aux îles Hébrides*, 3 vols (Paris/Genève: 1821).
2   F. C. Roe, 'La découverte de l'Ecosse entre 1760 et 1830', *Revue de littérature comparée*, 27 (1953), 59–75 (p. 69).

The long poem 'On a Raised Beach' (1934) is an evocation of the remoteness and the geology of the Shetland island of Whalsay. It was composed by Hugh MacDiarmid (1892–1978) and is a supreme example of his fusion of poetic and scientific insights; Necker de Saussure might have nodded assent:

> Here a man must shed the encumbrances that muffle
> Contact with elemental things, the subtleties
> That seem inseparable from a humane life, and go apart
> Into a simple and sterner, more beautiful and more
>   oppressive world,
> Austerely intoxicating …[3]

MacDiarmid could have been writing about the Swiss Alps – but that is the point: didacticism allied to a landscape, equally bleak and impressive, and tingling delight in it all. Austere intoxication is the characteristic of both Scottish and Swiss culture. In music, the Scot Sir Alexander Mackenzie's oratorio 'The Rose of Sharon' (1880s) is sensuous without becoming over-ripe for any incipient Wagnerism is held in check. The songs and operas of Othmar Shoeck (1886–1957) avoid Richard-Straussian excess: he knows exactly when to keep both melodiousness and dissonance under control. In architecture, Charles Rennie Mackintosh's masterpiece, the Glasgow School of Art (1897–1909), suggests *art nouveau* flowerings in strict equipoise with no-nonsense geometrics; Switzerland has its little-known *Jugendstil* buildings but they are not obtrusive which may explain why they are little-known. I have, for instance, enjoyed the dignified examples across the road from the railway station at Chiasso. Even the *Goetheanum* at Dornach, perhaps the most exotic building in Switzerland, has a dependable solidity about it, poised upon its hill.

Philippe-Sirice Bridel (1757–1845), latterly styled the 'Doyen' Bridel, was a pastor from the Canton of Vaud, an unlikely position,

---

3 Hugh MacDiarmid, *Complete Poems 1920–1976*, edited by Michael Grieve and W. R. Aitken, 2 vols (London: 1978), I, p. 428.

one would think, from which to make utterances of high cultural ambition. He sought to transcend the local cantonal scene by calling for a francophone poetry of Swiss national identity. In the course of the intellectual side of his mission, he drew on a wide range of interests – folklore, language, demography, botany and other sciences – and from 1783 published an annual almanac, the *Etrennes helvétiennes*.

Benjamin Constant, for one, was not impressed, dismissing Bridel as an 'homme assez instruit, mais très pedant et très lourd'.[4] Few would make great claims for Bridel's own poetry, collected in 1782 as *Poésies helvétiennes*. The preface, however, grandly titled 'Discours préliminaire sur la poésie nationale' offers a rationale for his procedure. Poetry, for Bridel, is above all visual, images are its essence. The true poetic images derive from nature, which is greater than man. Switzerland is blessed to be so rich in natural splendour, containing above all the Alps which of course dominate the country and would thus provide for Bridel a national rather than a narrowly cantonal focus.

A 'poésie nationale' of any country is based on the description of its landscapes and customs. Beyond Switzerland, Bridel finds examples of this in poets such as James Thomson (1700–48), author of *The Seasons*, and in Ossian, who was born just within Scotland, at Ednam near Kelso, and was educated at the University of Edinburgh. In 1725 he settled in London and his authorship of 'Rule Britannia' might throw us off the scent of any 'Scottishness' in his work. His evocations in 'Winter', however, are of a harsh northern climate, and its moralism is that of a Scottish clergyman's son. From his own perspective, this suits Bridel perfectly. 'Au lieu de la civilité & des petits soins,' he wrote, 'on trouvera en Suisse des restes de l'ancienne hospitalité; au lieu de la galanterie, du sentiment, & de la vertu au lieu de philosophie'.[5] Jean-Jacques Rousseau famously dismissed French

---

4   Benjamin Constant, *Ma vie, Ecrits littéraires (1800–1813)*, *Œuvres complètes* (Tübingen: 1995), III/1, p. 307.

5   Philippe-Sirice Bridel, *Poésies helvétiennes* (Lausanne: 1782), p. xiii.

sophistication in favour of Swiss wholesomeness and he would have
no theatre in Geneva. Bridel surpasses Rousseau in the sincerity of
his position for one cannot imagine him setting up an illicit love-nest
on the French side of the frontier.

In the course of 'Winter', Thomson describes an avalanche in the
Grisons, and this may have further commended him to Bridel. In the
latter's paraphrase of the poem, however, he restricts himself to its con-
clusion, where with Thomson he can call to account 'Ye vainly wise!
Ye blind presumptuous' // 'Vous sages orgueilleux, aveugles déguisés'
for the neglect of 'the lone widow and her orphans' // 'l'orphelin
pauvre & la veuve affligée'. Luxury 'in palaces' forms 'unreal wants'
// 'la paresse assise sous le dais / Au sein de l'abondance habite les
palais'.[6]

The stark moralism also informs Bridel's response to Ossian –
or rather to those prose pieces ostensibly by the third-century bard
of that name, but which were in fact the concoctions of that most
notorious of literary charlatans, James Macpherson (1736–96).
Throughout Europe it became commonplace to compare Homer and
Ossian as epic poets and Bridel concedes the sublimity of the former,
but he 'ne fut point un héros'. The Greek celebrates the exploits of
the ancestors of kings, his masters, but the 'Barde Écossais' sings the
exploits of his own ancestors, of his companions in arms, of his own
family: 'Tandis qu'Homère fait admirer son génie, Ossian inspire pour
lui-même l'attendrissement & le respect'.[7] Bridel cites an example
of how Ossian's warrior-heroes are more honourable than those of
Homer: whereas in Book 10 of *The Iliad* Ulysses and Diomed take
advantage of the slumbering Trojan camp in order to engage in mas-
sacre and horse-theft, in Ossian/Macpherson's poem 'Lathmon' it is
not worthy action to 'rush on the sleeping foe … [to] come like a
blast by night, when it overturns the young trees in secret' // 'fondre
sur un ennemi qui dort, … ressembler au vent furieux qui déracine

6   ibid, p. 13.
7   ibid, pp. 125–26.

en secret les jeunes arbres au milieu de la nuit'.[8] Bridel sees the 'anciens Écossais', like the Swiss, as mountain-dwellers, with an integrity to match the grandeur of their terrain. They are not distracted, he goes on, by the petty, frivolous concerns of those who inhabit the cities and the plains.

Whereas Bridel renders fragments of Macpherson's English prose into French prose, he resorts to rhyming couplets for his main translation activity in 'The Songs of Selma' which had appeared in a German translation by Goethe in his novel *Die Leiden des Jungen Werther* (1774). The narrative of Werther's doomed love for Charlotte, their soulful sharing of 'The Songs of the Selma' during their *soirées à deux*, and Werther's suicide, all appealed to a Europe smitten with the cult of sentiment. Many a young poseur bedecked himself in Werther's trademark of blue frock coat and yellow waistcoat. None of that has served to commend 'The Songs of Selma' to today's readers, but this cannot be put down entirely to guilt by association. At least one translator of Goethe's tale found Macpherson's text 'so weird and awkward it could never plausibly have moved Lotte and Werther to their tragic breakdown'. For Catherine Hutter Goethe's German version was far superior to the original, and she opted to re-translate it back into English.[9]

Macpherson – rather like Bridel himself – is important not so much for his intrinsic literary merit as for having initiated a cultural phenomenon for the Ossian craze spread throughout Europe. Even Napoleon carried a copy with him on his campaigns, a sure testament to Macpherson's gift for bombast. It did not necessarily require much literary skill to improve on Macpherson's originals, and one method was to turn the turgid prose into relatively livelier verse. Bridel's offering is in this respect somewhat more than serviceable, as with this elegiac passage:

8   ibid, pp. 129–30.
9   Johann Wolfgang von Goethe, *The Sorrows of Young Werther and Selected Writings*, translated by Catherine Hutter (New York: 1962), p. 252.

Thou were swift, O Morar! As a roe on the desert, terrible as a meteor of fire. Thy wrath was as the storm. Thy sword in battle, as lightning in the field. Thy voice was a stream after rain; like thunder on distant hills. Many fell by thy arm; they were consumed in the flames of thy wrath. But when thou didst return from war, how peaceful was thy brow! Thy face was like the sun after rain; like the moon in the silence of night; calm as the breast of the lake when the loud wind is laid.

Morar! tu t'élançais comme un cerf solitaire / Que poursuit de chasseurs une troupe légère; / La terreur & la mort accouraient avec toi, / Lorsque dans les combats semant par tout l'effroi, / Plus vite que l'éclair tu volais au carnage: / Ta voix était semblable au bruit qui dans l'orage / Gronde en perçant des cieux la vaste profondeur; / Plus d'un vaillant guerrier périt dans ta fureur: / Mais après le combat plus serein, plus paisible, / Tu n'avais plus cet air sanguinaire & terrible, / Pareil, après la foudre au soleil qui nous luit; / A la lune écartant les ombres de la nuit; / Calme comme ce lac quand l'aquilon rapide / Cesse de soulever sa surface limpide.[10]

Within the Central Belt of Scotland – the cities of Edinburgh and Glasgow, together with their hinterland – George Gordon, Lord Byron (1788–1824) is not generally considered to be a 'Scottish' poet. Further north, though, in Aberdeen and 'twal mile roun' (twelve miles round), the perspective changes. Abandoned by their husband and father, 'Mad Jack' Byron of Newstead Abbey, Lady Byron and young George were obliged to live in meaner circumstances in Aberdeen as Lady Byron had been Catherine Gordon of Gight, and thus belonged to the North-East. Young Byron absorbed the folklore and folksong of the area, variously echoed or remarked upon in the course of his poetry, not least in 'Don Juan' (1814–24), where he declares himself 'half a Scot by birth, and bred / A whole one'.[11]

10 *Poésies helvétiennes*, p. 145.
11 Byron, *Don Juan*, Canto the Tenth, stanza XVII: editions of Byron are various and widely available, so I have not opted to refer to one in particular.

The boy experienced Calvinist dogma (and sexual instruction) from a local nurse. Scottish Calvinism exercised a potent influence not only on its adherents but on all who came within the orbit of its culture. The doctrine of predestination and the consequent sense of inescapable doom; the Manichaean division of the populace into the Saved and the Damned; the 'justified sins' of the Saved who felt emboldened to commit any action, even murder, in the pursuit of supposedly godly ends – all that, and much else, was conducive to a psychology of split personality, of hypocritical actions and guilty feelings.

Byron's sojourns in Switzerland are well-documented, and his poem 'The Prisoner of Chillon' (1816) is iconic, but it is his verse drama *Manfred* (1817) which most powerfully evokes the Swiss mountain landscape in all its grandeur. The pre-Romanticism of Bridel has become the Romanticism of Byron, but the word 'Romanticism' must be deployed with caution in this context, not least because Byron's vestigially Calvinist pessimism is at odds with any Romantic belief in the boundless opportunities for individuals and nations. Byron of course was the champion of liberty for small European countries, notably Greece, but all bombast – even his own – is undercut by his dark, bitter humour. He was a master of satire, a genre practised not by revolutionaries but by those who take a dim view of humankind.

It is at least arguable that *Manfred* could not have been composed as it was by someone unaffected by Scottish Calvinism. Its eponymous hero, wracked with guilt for a hideous crime which is never specified, lives as an outcast in the Alps. It is true that, as an accomplished man who is yet subject to competing moral pressures, Manfred shares many of the attributes of Goethe's Faust. However, it is the sheer didactic energy of Manfred's self-analysis, which he places in a strong theological context, that marks him out as an Aberdonian contemplating the Jungfrau Mountain:

How beautiful is all this visible world!
How glorious in its action and itself!
But we, who name ourselves its sovereigns, we,
Half dust, half deity, alike unfit
To sink or soar, with our mix'd essence make
A conflict of our elements, and breathe
The breath of degradation and of pride,
Contending with low wants and lofty will,
Till our mortality predominates,
And men are – what they name not to themselves,
And trust not to each other.[12]

In Act 2, Scene 2, the Witch of the Alps addresses Manfred as
'a man of many thoughts, / And deeds of good and ill, extreme in
both, / Fatal and fated in thy sufferings'. A few lines later Manfred
launches into a speech where he declares his aloofness from the
common concerns of his fellow human beings, and his concomitant
identity with the Alps, their physical extremes matching his spiritual
extremes:

My joy was in the Wilderness, to breathe
The difficult air of the iced mountain's top,
Where the birds dare not build, nor insect's wing
Flit o'er the herbless granite; or to plunge
Into the torrent, and to roll along
On the swift whirl of the new breaking wave
Of river-stream, or ocean, in their flow.
In these my early strength exulted [...][13]

Manfred, then, is a seeker after 'austere intoxication', quite the opposite of the debonair sensuality to which Mephistopheles lures an
all-too-willing Faust.

The Scottish Calvinist energies of Thomas Carlyle (1795–1881)
are of a much less attractive nature, infused as they are with a bully-

---

12 Byron, *Manfred*, Act 1, Scene 2.
13 ibid, Act 2, Scene 2.

ing, Victorian self-righteousness. On the credit side, there is a forth-right integrity common to those Scots who are not ambitious and those Swiss who are not privy to dictators' bank accounts. Carlyle's formal studies at the University of Edinburgh were supplemented by much intense self-education, and his biographer Ian Campbell has noted his keen interest in the natural sciences as expounded in Swiss publications, notably the Geneva-based periodical the *Bibliothèque universelle*, whose numbers he would have consulted in Edinburgh University Library.[14]

More telling in the present context is what Carlyle has to say in his first published monograph on Schiller's last play; for obvious reasons, *Wilhelm Tell* is effectively an honorary Swiss work. In his *Life of Friedrich Schiller* (1825) Carlyle takes the opportunity, as a man of Scottish peasant stock, to salute his Swiss counterparts, who in 1291 were the founders of the Helvetian Confederation. There is almost an echo of the Doyen Bridel in Carlyle's praise for the play's subject matter: 'An air of freshness and wholesomeness breathes over it; we are among honest, inoffensive, yet fearless peasants, untainted by the vices, undazzled by the theories, of more complex and per-verted conditions of society'.[15] Those Swiss freedom-fighters, he goes on, are not 'speculative patriots [...] they never mention the Social Contract, or the Rights of Man. [...] The rules by which they steer are not deduced from remote premises, by a fine process of thought; they are the accumulated result of experience, transmitted from peasant sire to peasant son'.[16] Carlyle was the highly subjective histor-ian of *The French Revolution* (1837), where he thunders against the abstract, ideological nature of the upheaval in Paris. Ever the critic

---

14 Ian Campbell, *Thomas Carlyle*, paperback edition (Edinburgh: 1993), p. 41; Ian Campbell, 'Correspondence between Scotland, England and Switzerland', in *Nationalism in Literature*, edited by Horst Drescher and Hermann Völkel (Frankfurt am Main: 1989), pp. 237–56.

15 Thomas Carlyle, *The Life of Friedrich Schiller*, Centenary Edition [of] the Works of Thomas Carlyle, vol. 25 (London: 1899), p. 174.

16 ibid., pp. 174–75.

of the mechanical nature of British industrialism and of the mindset
which it induced, Carlyle attacks Robespierre's new religion of the
Supreme Being as an all too 'conscious Mumbo-Jumbo' which 'knows
that it is machinery'. Carlyle is cognisant that Robespierre's ideology
derives from Rousseau's political theories, but this is Rousseau in
French, rather than Swiss mode, and Carlyle is no admirer of France.
For him French culture is variously superficial and frivolous, icono-
clastic and rationalist; he prefers Germanic values with their stress on
duty and spiritual idealism, and it is an essentially Germanic Swit-
zerland, via Schiller, which he celebrates in his account of Wilhelm
Tell. Switzerland is sometimes called the 'America' of Europe, and the
'Swiss Revolution', as Carlyle calls it, was as pragmatic as the French
Revolution was dogmatic. By analogy, the American Revolution,
while not lacking its philosophical bearings (there is the example of
Jefferson), was markedly less ideological than that of the French.

Carlyle's discussion of *Wilhelm Tell* incorporates his own translation of Act 4, Scene 3, which includes Tell's assassination of Gessler,
the tyrannical Austrian governor, precipitating 'the final triumph
and liberation of the Swiss'. Carlyle's version is in stiff, unmemorable
English blank verse; however, there is a significant repetition, in his
concluding critical remarks, of four lines of the translation that has
gone before:

> Ein armer
> Wildheuer, gutter Herr, vom Rigiberge,
> Der überm Abgrund weg das freie Gras
> Abmähet von den schroffen Felsenwänden,
> Wohin das Vieh sich nicht getraut zu steigen –
>
> The poor wild-hay-man of the Rigiberg,
> Whose trade is, on the brow of the abyss,
> To mow the common grass from craggy shelves
> And nooks to which the cattle dare not climb, –

To Carlyle, this is one of the points at which 'we stand as if in
presence of the Swiss, beholding the achievement of their freedom

in its minutest circumstances, with all its simplicity and unaffected greatness'.[17]

In 1830 Carlyle made a translation of J. P. F. Richter's review of Madame de Staël's *De l'Allemagne*. This was a fitting venture, for as de Staël was the Swiss who introduced German literature to a francophone readership so Carlyle was the Scot who did likewise for the English-speaking world. The Swiss and the Scots have in common an internationalism that acts as a foil to their often parochial isolation, enabling them to act as intermediaries between cultures.

In this respect, Sir Walter Scott (1771–1832) serves as a precursor of Carlyle. Scott's earliest writings engage with German literature: he translated Goethe's drama *Götz von Berlichingen* in 1799, and thereby set the scene for his original work in the neo-medieval romance and the historical novel. His versions of German ballads included 'The Battle of Sempach', based, as he tells us, on a piece by a Lucerne shoemaker-poet called Albert Tchudi. The battle in question was fought in July 1386, and the ballad celebrates the valour of the Swiss against the Austrians, and in particular that of the iconic self-sacrificing hero Winkelried.

Some thirty years later, Scott revisited Switzerland but in imagination only for he confessed that he had never set foot in the country. In 1829 appeared his novel *Anne of Geierstein*, the action of which takes place during the English Wars of the Roses and the ongoing political-military intrigues between England, France and Burgundy. The Earl of Oxford and his son Arthur de Vere are travelling *incognito* in mainland Europe, intent on seeking support for the Lancastrian cause at a time when the rival Yorkist party is in power. While in Switzerland they are caught up in a mountain storm and are accorded shelter and hospitality by the *Landamman* – a kind of ruling magistrate – of the Canton of Unterwalden. His niece, Anne of Geierstein, saves the life of Arthur, who is unaccustomed to

17 ibid., p. 186; the translation occupies pp. 177–86.

negotiating the precipitous route leading to the castled peak of the *Landamman*. Anne, a robust Swiss maid equally unaccustomed to vertigo, coaxes Arthur over to her verge of the ravine which divides them. Arthur feels no little unmanliness in having owed his life to a woman, but it all proves to be the dramatic beginning to an encounter that will assuredly develop into love.

It is as if Scott echoes Carlyle in viewing Swiss strength of character as epitomised by footsureness in 'nooks to which the cattle dare not climb'. He goes on to represent other national attributes in the person of the *Landamman* and his niece. Anne's father, the brother of *Landamman*, has opted to retain the family's aristocratic German status which has been renounced by the *Landamman* himself who, for his part, has passed on his unpretentious Swiss values to his niece. The *Landamman* enunciates to his English guests his preference for '"the village dance"' to '"the feasts of German nobles"', together with his republican pride in '"the home-bred virtues of the Romans"' while rejecting '"their lust of conquest and love of foreign luxuries"'. Much later in the novel, in the course of an address to the Burgundian court, he declares that the free Swiss would prefer starvation '"in the icy wastes of the glaciers"' to domination by a foreign power.[18]

Were it not that much else proceeds at a fast pace in this novel of six hundred pages, the sententiousness of the *Landamman* could become more than a little wearisome. Scott's admiration for the hardy ways of Scottish Highland chieftains such as Rob Roy has become transposed to a Swiss counterpart. This author, however, is a Tory who cannot himself accept the blanket dismissal by the *Landamman* of aristocratic values which, after all, include a certain grace, loyalty, and sense of responsibility, eminently displayed by his English visitors. The simpering decadence of the Provençal court (lightly sketched

---

18 Sir Walter Scott, *Anne of Geierstein*, New Century Library [edition of] the Works of Sir Walter Scott, Bart., vol. 23 (London: 1906), pp. 69, 103, 528–29; see also Thomas R. Dale, 'Anne of Geierstein: a Political Testament', *Scottish Literary Journal*, 7 (1980), 193–201.

towards the end of Chapter 32) is not the whole story. Anne herself, despite her uncle's tutelage, takes no little delight in the baronial status which she inherits from her father, and is indeed happy to unite in her person the best in the divergent value-systems of her two elders: '"Thou shalt see me behave as becomes both a German lady and a Swiss maiden"'.[19]

In *Anne of Geierstein* Scott evokes the Swiss mountainscape without, of course, ever having seen it for himself. This does not prevent him from contrasting the 'gloomy and threatening' aspect of Mount Pilatus with the gentler, sunlit range of Rigi. At the beginning of the novel Scott remarks of the time in which the action is set: 'It was not an age in which the beauties or grandeur of a landscape made much impression either on the minds of those who travelled through the country or who resided in it'.[20] How different are attitudes at the time when he is writing the novel, and indeed Scott himself is largely responsible for the early nineteenth-century admiration of landscape for its own sake. With the European success of his poem 'The Lady of the Lake' (1810), Scott in effect created the Scottish tourist industry. Indeed, according to Amédée Pichot (1795–1877), who translated Scott's poetry into French, the Switzerland of William Tell had found a rival in the Scotland of William Wallace; pilgrims to Loch Katrine – the setting for The Lady of the Lake – had become as numerous as those bound for Lake Geneva.[21] For the purposes of translation, the two countries could be conveniently interchanged, as when August Corrodi (1826–1885) turned the poems of Robert Burns from Scots into 'Schwytzerdütsch':

> Till a' the seas gang dry, my dear,
> And the rocks melt wi' the sun:
> And I will luve thee still, my dear,
> While the sands o' life shall run.

19 *Anne of Geierstein*, p. 349.
20 ibid, p. 6.
21 L.A. Bisson, *Amédée Pichot: a Romantic Prometheus* (Oxford: n.d.), p. 329.

De Rhi mag trichne, de Rigi mag
I heisser sunn vergah :
Ich ha min schatz lieb bis emal
Mi letzti stund wird schla.[22]

Robert Louis Stevenson (1850–94), a frail man subject to doctor's orders, arrived at the health resort of Davos during the autumn of 1880, and found his stay long on austerity but short on intoxication. Even he, however, admitted that the mountains could offer a bit of both: 'In many ways it is a trying business to reside upon the Alps [...] But one thing is undeniable – that is, in the rare air, clear, cold and blinding light of Alpine winters, a man takes a certain *troubled delight* in his existence which can nowhere else be paralleled. He is perhaps no happier, but he is *stingingly alive*'.[23] The deployment of oxymoron comes naturally to the author of that iconic study of duality, *The Strange Case of Dr Jekyll and Mr Hyde* (1886).

During its previous Geneva-based incarnation, the *Bibliothèque universelle* had featured many Scottish authors, including Walter Scott, whose poetry and fiction appeared there in French translation. During the 1860s the journal merged with the *Revue suisse* and the resulting new *Bibliothèque universelle* moved to Lausanne. It was consciously Swiss and opposed to French literary movements such as Naturalism and Symbolism, which it viewed as respectively reductive and decadent. It boycotted the work of the Swiss writer Edouard Rod (1857–1910) during his too 'parisiané' alignment with Zola and Naturalism, admitting him to its pages once he had made a recantation. It is in this context that one can appreciate the response of Auguste Glardon, a regular contributor to the *Bibliothèque universelle*, to the work of Robert Louis Stevenson (himself a vocal opponent of Zola) and his Scottish contemporaries J. M. Barrie,

22 *Lieder von Robert Burns*, in das Schweizerdeutsche übertragen von August Corrodi (Zürich: 1971), pp. 48–49.

23 Robert Louis Stevenson, 'Swiss Notes', in his *Further Memories*, Tusitala Edition (London: 1923), p. 155; the italics are mine.

S. R. Crockett and 'Ian Maclaren' (Dr John Watson). In Scotland itself, the last three were to become identified as the 'kailyard' school, and would be accused of sentimentally evading the realities of Scottish urban life. As a Swiss who had studied theology in Edinburgh and who wrote for evangelical outlets, Glardon was eminently predisposed towards the wholesome values espoused by the Scottish writers. Yet Glardon's criticism, for all its piety, could not be dismissed as facile or hypocritical. He considers Stevenson's Mr Hyde – the 'evil' double of Dr Jekyll – to be 'un triste personnage'; Jekyll, for all his outward virtue, is only too ready to give free rein to his alter ego and then 'dormir tranquille'. As for Long John Silver in *Treasure Island*, Glardon stresses the moral complexity of Stevenson's famously attractive rogue, suggesting that in similar circumstances others would probably behave no better. And in a long exposition of Stevenson's essay 'The Lantern Bearers', Glardon is in accord with the Scot's defence of children's natural creativity, which equips them for their duty to others. Glardon's moralism, like Stevenson's, is antipuritanical: he turns the tables on the Zolaesque Naturalists who profess to be so free and frank about sex and other *bourgeois* taboos; Stevenson is right to take them to task, because it is they who are the true killjoy puritans with their 'horizon étroit et de courte vue'.[24]

---

24   For Glardon on Scottish writers see, passim, his articles in the *Bibliothèque universelle et Revue suisse* (Lausanne: 1862–1924): 'A travers la littérature anglaise contemporaine: Les romans', vol. 54 (1892), 532–35 only, continued in vol. 55 (1892), 516–20, 526–27, 538–47 only; 'Robert-Louis Stevenson', vol. 66 (1895), 493–521, continued in vol. 67 (1895), 80–111; 'Un nouvel humoriste écossais: Jan [i.e. Ian] Maclaren', vol. 1 [new series] (1896), 564–86; 'Un Gavroche écossais' on S.R. Crockett, and in particular his novel *Cleg Kelly*, vol. 3 (1896), 530–62; 'Le nouveau livre [i.e. *Margaret Ogilvy*] de J.M. Barrie', vol. 6 (1897), 67–95. There is also a sympathetic review, in vol. 8 (1897), 641–42, of Ian Maclaren's article 'Ugliness in Fiction', which had appeared in the review *Literature*, I (1897), 80–101; Maclaren had condemned incipient Zolaism in English fiction: 'There are such things as drains, and sometimes they may have to be opened, but one

As twentieth-century modernism made its eventual impact on Scotland and Switzerland, there was a lessening in the exchange of provincial pieties. Worthiness was no longer held in esteem. On the Swiss side, the key figure is Eugen Gomringer (b. 1925), the leading instigator of the Concrete Poetry movement. Here we have a poetry which rejects traditional diction in favour of sheer play – the poet as *homo ludens* – and of the visual importance of the words on the page. In Scotland, Edwin Morgan (b. 1920) played a like role; a collection of his own concrete poetry, *Starryveldt*, was published in 1965 by the Eugen Gomringer Press of Frauenfeld, Switzerland, he has made translations of Gomringer's work and French versions of Morgan's poetry have since appeared in the Lausanne-based review, *Écriture*.[25] The origin of Concrete Poetry can be traced back to the *Calligrammes* (1918) of the French poet Guillaume Apollinaire, to whose avant-garde circle belonged Blaise Cendrars (1887–1961), Swiss-born, part-Scottish, but above all a wandering cosmopolitan. Donny O'Rourke (b. 1959), like Morgan a poet who manages to be both Glaswegian and international in his bearings, has turned a number of Cendrars's poems into Glaswegian Scots, in his versions opting for a relocation from Paris – 'An thon's thi wey Ah stravaig Glesca ilka nicht, / Frae Kelvinbrig tae thi Calton'.[26]

In the same year as O'Rourke's *Cendrars* (1996), the July issue of the Swiss literary magazine *orte* consisted largely of a Scottish poetry feature, 'Brücke nach Edinburgh'. Poets including Ron Butlin, Stewart Conn, Norman MacCaig and Tessa Ransford appeared in German translation. This publication in part motivated me to initiate a trans-lation project in the other direction and the results were two guest-

would not for choice have one opened in his library', (art. cit.); see also *La "Bibliothèque universelle" (1815–1924): miroir de la sensibilité romande au XIXe siècle*, publié sous la direction de Yves Bridel et Roger Francillon (Lausanne: 1998).

25 *Écriture* [printemps 1998], 95–109.

26 'In thi Warld's Hert' (from Cendrars's 'Au cœur du monde') in Donny O'Rourke and Richard Price, *Eftirs / Afters* (Glasgow: 1996), p. [8].

editorships: firstly, of the Hairst 2001 issue of the magazine *Lallans*, in which I printed Scots versions by a number of poet-translators of Swiss work originally in French, German, Italian and Romansch; and secondly, of the Autumn 2002 issue of the magazine *Fife Lines*. Mindful of his recent versions of Baudelaire in Scots, I invited James Robertson to tackle Louis Duchosal (1862–1901), a rare Swiss example of decadent, fin-de-siècle sensibility: 'Comme sous les gibets, de pales mandragores / A mes pieds où le sang suintait de tous les pores'. // 'As if ablow a gibbet, pale mandrakes snurled roun / Ma feet whaur aw ma life's bluid sypit doun'.[27] After a public reading of his Duchosal, James remarked 'If that's not Swiss Symbolism, I don't know what is'.

If the old 'wholesomeness' was being challenged, perhaps the 'worthiness' was returning in a new form; if so, I plead guilty, as I wanted a representation, in *Lallans* and *Fife Lines*, of Swiss-Italian and Romansch poetry as a counterfoil to the domination of French and German. Romansch seemed particularly apt for make-overs into Scots to express the solidarity of Europe's 'lesser-used' languages. I was fortunate to secure the services of Christopher Whyte, equally brilliant as poet and linguist, for the work of Fabio Pusterla (b. 1957): 'Antiche scale / le scale di Albogasio, su cui passano / ilari i vivi e i morti, salutandosi piano'. // 'the stairs of Albogasio / are ancient stairs, and up and down them go / the quick and the dead, cheerful, murmuring greetings'.[28]

Finally, an apparent (if only apparent) symmetry: Regi Claire (b. 1962) is a Swiss writer living in Scotland; Peter McCarey (b. 1956) is a Scottish writer living in Switzerland. Claire, who is married to Ron Butlin, has produced a book of short stories, *Inside-Outside* (1998)

27 Saint-Sebastian/Saint Sebastian', *Lallans*, no. 59 (Hairst 2001), 28, 30.
28 'Movimenti ascensionali: le scale di Albogasio / movements in Ascent: the Stairs at Albogasio', *Fife Lines*, no. 6 (Autumn 2002), 88–89; Romansch and Scottish Gaelic are brought together on a British Council-sponsored CD, *Cara: Alive and Rocking / Viver e Far Vibrar / Beòis Beòthail / Beo Brìomhar* (no date; early 2000s).

and a novel, *The Beauty Room* (2002). Her portrayal of gutsy, rebellious women, and of sinister or subversive forces disturbing a bland, *bourgeois* order, has implications for both her countries. McCarey achieved an all-too-rare synthesis of Scottish and comparative literary studies in his book *Hugh MacDiarmid and the Russians* (1987). His poetry's strength, however, is intellectual rather than academic; one may doubt that a university career would have served him as well as his post as a translator with the World Health Organisation in Geneva. Switzerland as such features rarely in his work as a writer, though he has commented perceptively on the multilingual, and therefore multiliterary, phenomena in both the countries of his birth and his residence. His poem 'GVA' coolly juxtaposes neutral, international Geneva with immediately neighbouring French territory to the southeast, a centre of resistance during World War Two: 'for history has passed you by / in Nazi gliders closing on Glières / with the traffic in diplomatic plate / you give yourself to me Geneva / no one has loved you like this since Lord Byron. / Slut'.[29]

Two centuries on from our starting-point, literary travellers may or may not be as rapturous as they were – they are certainly much less naïve.

29 Peter McCarey, *In the Metaforest* (London: 2000), p. 8. Peter McCarey's essays are available online at <http://www.thesyllabary.com/FindAngel-Contents.htm>.

Malcolm Pender

August Corrodi's Contribution to Perceptions of Robert Burns in Nineteenth-century German-speaking Europe[1]

In 1870 the Swiss writer, poet and painter August Corrodi (1826–1885) published a selection of the songs of Robert Burns translated into 'das Schweizerdeutsche'.[2] Nine years previously, Corrodi had written for the journal *Die Schweiz* an appreciation of Burns and the southern German poet and writer Johann Peter Hebel (1760–1826), an essay published in book form in 1873.[3] I set my discussion both of Corrodi's thirty-year involvement with Burns and of his translations (the only ones to date into Swiss dialect)[4] in the context of the awareness of Burns in German-speaking Europe in the nineteenth century and of the problems encountered by his German translators.

1 I am grateful to Dr Andrew Noble for his help as I was writing this article.

2 August Corrodi, *Lieder von Robert Burns, ins Schweizerdeutsche übertragen* (Winterthur: Bleuler-Hausheer, 1870); L in the text with page references to the edition published in 1998 by the Althea Verlag, Zürich.

3 August Corrodi, 'Robert Burns und Peter Hebel. Eine literar-historische Parallele', *Die Schweiz. Illustrierte Zeitschrift für Literatur und Kunst*, nos. 1 and 2 (1861); published in book form with minor changes as August Corrodi, *Rob. Burns und Pet. Hebel. Eine literar-historische Parallele* (Berlin: Lüdert'sche Buchhandlung, 1873) ; B in the text with page references.

4 Hans Jürg Kupper, *Robert Burns im deutschen Sprachraum* (Bern: Francke Verlag, 1979), p. 69; anyone writing on this topic must be indebted to this wide-ranging and illuminating study.

The earliest translations of individual songs or poems by Burns into German appeared in miscellanies, the first by Bothe in 1795 during the poet's lifetime, and among those which followed was one in 1801 by the illustrious and influential figure of Herder. Such perception of Burns as there was in Germany during the first quarter of the nineteenth century derived principally from Emilie von Berlepsch's four-volume account of a year spent in Scotland, *Caledonia*, published in Hamburg between 1802 and 1804.[5] As might be expected of someone who had gone to Scotland in search of Ossian, her portrait, although sympathetic, is somewhat highly-coloured, focussing on Burns as a 'Naturgenie'. However, the decisive event which 'marks the dawn of Burns's fame in Germany'[6] was the mention of Burns in 1830 in Goethe's introduction to the German translation of Thomas Carlyle's *Life of Schiller*. Three years previously, in a conversation recorded by Eckermann, Goethe had expressed an understanding of the power of the Scottish poet with his strong links to a living folk tradition:

> Nehmen Sie Burns. Wodurch ist er groß, als daß die alten Lieder seiner Vorfahren im Munde des Volkes lebten, daß sie ihm sozusagen bei der Wiege gesungen wurden, daß er als Knabe unter ihnen heran wuchs und die hohe Vortrefflichkeit dieser Muster sich ihm einlebte, daß er darin eine lebendige Basis hatte, worauf er weiterschreiten konnte. Und ferner wodurch ist er groß, als daß seine eigenen Lieder in seinem Volke sogleich empfängliche Ohren fanden.[7]

Now, reacting to a letter from Carlyle in the autumn of 1828 which announced the plan for an 'Essay on Burns' and in which Carlyle

---

5   Kupper, p.14; see also Hans Utz, *Schotten und Schweizer – Brother Mountaineers. Europa entdeckt die beiden Völker im 18. Jahrhundert* (Bern: Peter Lang, 1995), p.15.

6   Hans Hecht, 'The Reception of Burns in German Literature', *Burns Chronicle and Club Directory*, Second Series, XIV (1939), 52–60 (p. 54).

7   Johan Peter Eckermann, *Gespräche mit Goethe in den letzten Jahren seines Lebens* (Reutlingen: Bertelsmann, 1960), p. 446 (3 May 1827).

conjectured that Goethe might not have heard of Burns, Goethe can truthfully say: 'Mehr jedoch als unser Freund vermuthen mochte, war uns Robert Burns bekannt'.[8] He goes on to recommend Lockhart's *The Life of Robert Burns* (1828) to his German readers and closes his remarks on Burns by associating himself with Carlyle's praise: 'Auch wir rechnen den belobten Robert Burns zu den ersten Dichtergeistern, welche das vergangene Jahrhundert hervorgebracht hat'.[9]

In the 1830s a third well-known German, the poet Ferdinand Freiligrath, showed an interest in Burns by publishing several highly-regarded translations of songs and in 1854 managed, in the third year of his long political exile in Britain, to meet an aged sister of the poet.[10] At the end of the 1830s came the first collections of translations in book form: Philipp Kaufmann's *Gedichte von Robert Burns* (1839), Wilhelm Gerhard's *Robert Burns' Gedichte* (1840) and Heinrich Julius Heintze's *Lieder und Balladen des Schotten Robert Burns* (1840), this last volume being favourably noticed by Carlyle who wrote in his 1840 review that 'Herr Heintze has done his task in a decidedly creditable manner'.[11] After 1840, there was a fairly steady production of editions throughout the remainder of the nineteenth century and it is worthwhile mentioning some publications centring round the centenaries of Burns's birth (1859) and death (1896).

Georg Pertz published *Lieder von Robert Burns* in 1859 and in the same year Heintze brought out a second edition, *Robert Burns' Gedichte*, a 'Markstein in der Geschichte der Burns-Übersetzung'[12] because it contained so much material which was new to a German

---

8   Einleitung zu Thomas Carlyle, *Leben Schillers*, reprinted in Thomas Carlyle, *The Life of Friedrich Schiller* (London: Chapman and Hall, 1885), pp. 289–302 (p. 294).

9   ibid, p. 297.

10 Kupper, p. 179.

11 Samuel Arthur Jones (ed.), *Collectanea Thomas Carlyle 1821–1855* (Canton, Penn.: Kirges, 1903), pp. 99–106 (pp. 100–101).

12 Kupper, p. 32.

audience, showing that his scope was wider than a writer of songs and ballads. In 1896, the main publication, amongst the many essays in his honour, was fittingly the largest anthology to date of translations, Wilhelmine Prinzhorn's *Lieder und Balladen von Robert Burns nebst einer Auswahl der Gedichte*, which contained some 111 of her own translations as well as 220 items by 34 other translators.[13] Already, two years before the appearance of Prinzhorn's book, tribute had been paid to German activity since 'over a score of more or less competent translators have produced versions [...] adapted to the tunes with which the songs are identified in the original'.[14] In the centenary year William Jacks, in his *Robert Burns in Other Tongues*, wished 'to show how widely the influence of Burns has spread'[15] and devoted almost a third of his book to translations into German, by far the largest group in his review. This influence might, in Germany at least, have been based on doubtful perceptions since, as late as 1920, the claim was being made that sales of the Reclam edition of Burns, which comprised translations first published in 1869 and some parts of which were savaged by Jacks,[16] 'show the hold our great Scottish poet has had on the German people'.[17]

13 ibid, p. 42.

14 J. Young, 'Translations of Burns', *Burnsiana*, vol. 4, 1894, 40–42 (p. 40).

15 William Jacks, *Robert Burns in Other Tongues. A Critical Review of the Translations of the Songs & Poems of Robert Burns* (Glasgow: MacLehose, 1896), p. viii; the William Jacks Chair of German at the University of Glasgow was established in 1919 and endowed in part with a gift from Jacks's legacy; I wish to thank Dr Gordon Anderson for information on Jacks.

16 The translation of 'Tam o' Shanter' is characterised as 'the very acme of absurdity', Jacks, p. 46; see also Kupper, pp. 35–36 and p. 185 for comments on the Reclam translations and for as full a reconstruction of the history of the edition as is compatible with lost and destroyed records of the Reclam Verlag.

17 William Mackintosh, 'Burns in Germany', *The Kinross Advertiser*, 31 January 1920; the essay was later published in a slightly expanded form and with the addition of a bibliography in William Mackintosh, *Burns in*

An additional and important dimension to the reception of Burns in German-speaking Europe in the nineteenth century was the scholarly research conducted on his work. As early as 1846 Eduard Fiedler's two-volume *Geschichte der volksthümlichen schottischen Lieder-Dichtung* set Burns within the context of Scottish poetry and indicated his relationship to Scottish folk-song.[18] In 1859, Albert Traeger, in his biographical sketch of Burns seeks in two ways to correct a popular perception: firstly, he rejects as demeaning for him the categories 'Naturdicher' and 'Volksdichter', the former because it creates 'im Freistaate des Geistes Rangclassen und Kasten-Unter-schiede, Arisotkratie und Pöbel' and the latter invents 'das Proletariat des Parnassus'; secondly, he reviews critically the books of translations which have appeared to date, reserving his most acerbic comments for the first, that of Kaufmann, which is 'eine entsprechende Fort-setzung der Mißhandlungen, mit denen der arme Burns bei Lebzeiten gepeinigt wurde'.[19] In 1877 Carl and Alfons Kissner published their four-volume *Burns Album. 100 Lieder und Balladen mit ihren schot-tischen National-Melodien*, the culmination of their research into publications of Scottish folksongs. In the introduction they state, mindful of Carlyle's claim that 'the tune is always the soul of a song',[20] that their publication is restoring 'die Einheit von Wort und Klang'[21] absent from the many versions of Burns available in Germany. In 1899 Heinrich Molenaar returned to the word 'Naturdichter' which, according to him, distorts a proper understanding, firstly, of Burns and secondly, of artistic tradition. Molenaar points to the fact 'dass

Germany. Scoto-German Studies (Aberdeen: Milne and Henderson, 1928), pp. 1–33.

18   See Kupper, pp. 26–28 for a discussion of Fiedler's work.

19   Albert Traeger, 'Robert Burns', in Georg Pertz, *Lieder von Robert Burns. Mit einer biographischen Skizze von Albert Traeger* (Leipzig/Heidelberg: C. F. Winter'sche Verlagshandlung, 1859), pp. vi–lvi (p. x, p. xi, pp. liv–lv).

20   Jones, p. 101.

21   Quoted by Kupper, pp. 36–37.

sich in seinen [Burns's] Werken nicht weniger als etwa 200 Namen
mehr oder minder bedeutender Dichter und Schriftsteller verzeich-
net finden, zu denen er in irgend welcher Beziehung stand, oder
mit deren Werken er vertraut war'; as evidence of Burns's conscious
art, he quotes from the letter of 6 December 1792 to Mrs Dunlop:
'I pick up favourite quotations and store them in my mind as ready
armour',[22] a quotation cited nearly one hundred and sixty years later
when it is claimed, specifically of the song 'John Anderson my Jo'
but clearly with wider import: 'All is natural, obvious, and just – so
deceptively unconstrained that Burns the craftsman is likely to be
overlooked'.[23] Molenaar's statement, 'Auch das grösste Genie saugt
seine schöpferische Kraft nicht aus den Wurzeln des Waldes, sondern
es bedarf einer vorbereitenden Entwicklung, um diese dann zu ihrer
höchsten Höhe führen zu können',[24] was taken up by Otto Ritter at
the beginning of the twentieth century when he stated that Burns's
work 'durchaus aus litterarischen Anregungen hevorgewachsen ist'
and continued:

> Seine schottischen Volkslieder wurzeln im Boden der schottischen
> Volkslyrik, seine schottischen Gedichte knüpfen an die Tradition der
> 'Vernacular School' an, seine englischen Lieder und Gedichte stehen
> mehr oder minder unter dem Bann des (Pseudo-)Classicismus; über-
> dies hat die englische Kunstpoesie des 18. Jahrhunderts stark auf ihm
> gewirkt.[25]

22 Heinrich Molenaar, *Robert Burns' Beziehungen zur Litteratur*, (Erlangen/
    Leipzig: Deichert'sche Verlagsbuchhandlung, 1899), pp. xiii–xiv; almost a
    century later, Kenneth Simpson is again re-defining the notion of Burns as
    a 'Naturdichter' and cites the same quotation, Kenneth Simpson, 'Robert
    Burns: "Heaven-taught ploughman"?', in Kenneth Simpson (ed.), *Burns
    Now* (Edinburgh: Cannongate Academic, 1994), pp.71–91 (pp. 73–74).
23 Robert D. Thornton (ed.), *The Tuneful Flame. Songs of Robert Burns as He
    Sang Them* (Laurence: University of Kansas Press, 1957), p. 7.
24 Molenaar, p. 105.
25 Otto Ritter, *Quellenstudien zu Robert Burns. 1773–1791* (Berlin: Mayer &
    Müller, 1901), p. i.

Ritter's statement is perhaps also a fitting summary of the work of the scholars who have gone before him, to whom he elsewhere paid tribute, and it is sad to read a Burns scholar claiming fifty years later: 'Today Otto Ritter's work is gathering dust'.[26]

Transposing important literature from one language into another is, as William Jacks stated, vital work: 'Great minds are the common property of nations, and it would bring an eclipse on literature did translations cease'.[27] Burns was perceived in 1894 to pose particular problems to translators: 'Few authors present greater difficulties than those to be found in the pages of the works of our national poet'.[28] Indeed, in the same year, another critic, having dismissed translation of Burns into French as 'an impossibility' and having found 'Teutonic translations' not 'altogether satisfactory', went on to ask: 'Is it even possible to translate Burns's Scottish songs into English?'[29] Certainly, Germans were from an early point recording the difficulty for them of the language in which Burns wrote. In the first volume of her *Caledonia*, Emilie von Berlepsch asserts: 'Wir können sie [Burns's poems] in Deutschland nicht verstehen, da sie in der Mundart abgefasst sind, die man broad Scottish nennt.'[30] Thirty years later Goethe, in his introduction to Carlyle's *Leben Schillers*, complained of his reading of Burns: 'Wir bedauerten, dass uns die Schottische Sprache gerade da hinderlich war, wo er [Burns] des reinsten natürlichsten Ausdrucks sich gewiss bemächtigt

---

26 Robert D. Thornton, 'Robert Burns and Scottish Folk Song', *Scots Chronicle*, 1951, 62–68 (p. 62).

27 Jacks, p. xvi.

28 John Muir, 'Burns in German', *The Scots Magazine*, XIII (February 1894), 229–237 (p. 231).

29 Young, p. 42; Young was clearly unaware of the great achievement of Auguste Angellier, *Robert Burns: la vie et les œuvres*, 2 vols (Paris: 1893), a work which Jacks, p. 433, praises as 'a monument alike to poet and translator'; the *Catalogue* (1996) of the Burns Collection in the Mitchell Library, Glasgow, lists three translations into English: 1892, 1954 and 1990.

30 Quoted by Kupper, p. 56.

hatte'.[31] Clearly, the view expressed blithely ninety years afterwards that 'the poems of Burns are familiar to many in Germany and [...] the language difficulty is hardly any barrier to their perfect enjoyment',[32] is an aberrant one.

The problems for translators exist on three levels. Firstly, it is easy to misunderstand the original. Adolf Laun, for example, in his 1869 translation of 'The Cotter's Saturday Night' understands the line 'the haelsome parritch, chief o' Scotia's food' to refer to 'partridge' and renders it as 'Mit einem Rebhuhn, wie es den Scotten frommt'.[33] Secondly, there is the very much more complex problem of rendering rhythms in the target language. In the view of Kupper, German translators in the nineteenth century failed to tackle this task because they were too fixated by the perceived necessity to create rhymes: 'Nur zu oft sahen sie im Reim die Essenz aller Poesie und verwechselten übersetzerische Treue mit Reimhörigkeit'.[34] Thirdly, there is the complexity of the language of Burns. If it is true that Burns bestowed on his dialect, 'hitherto only despised and laughed at [...] a kind of classical dignity',[35] it is also true that what he wrote was in fact much more a composite language consisting of an adaptation of elements of written English to the spoken dialect of Ayrshire so it is an amalgam reminiscent of Gotthelf's adaptation of High German to Swiss-German in his novels. Thus some German translators believed that the problems could best be solved by rendering Burns's songs and poems into German dialect.[36] Certainly the Swiss August Corrodi was strongly convinced of the affinity between German-Swiss dialect and the language of Burns as his introduction to the Lieder, discussed below, makes clear.

31 Einleitung, p. 294.
32 Mackintosh, op. cit., 31 January 1920.
33 Cited by Young, p. 41; Jacks cites further examples of mistranslations.
34 Kupper, p. 33.
35 Hecht, p. 57.
36 See Kupper, pp. 58–61.

Born in Zürich in 1826, Corrodi followed family tradition by beginning in 1845 the study of theology at the universities of Zürich and Basel. Two years later, however, he abandoned theology and enrolled at the School of Art in Munich from which he graduated in 1851. There followed a period of twelve years, firstly in Sankt Gallen and then in Winterthur, during which he painted and wrote, publishing the first of many picture books for children in 1853 and travelling extensively within Switzerland and in northern Italy. In 1859 he became a mason and in 1862 he was appointed teacher of drawing for the senior secondary schools in Winterthur, a post which he held until his retirement in 1881 and during the tenure of which he continued to write, paint and draw. At his death in 1885, he had published, in addition to his books for children, two novels, several plays and much occasional writing.

Corrodi claimed, as has been indicated, that his interest in Burns stretched over a thirty-year period. Certainly, his papers contain drafts of translations of individual Burns poems which can be dated to the 1850s and there is a note of 3 October 1858: 'In der letzten woche hatt' ich mich mit übersetzungen aus Robert Burns beschäftigt und vieles gelang mir in unsere Mundart zu übertragen'.[37] Almost exactly two years later, he wrote to a friend: 'Meine Studien zu Robert Burns führen mich auf ganz neue pfade und ich glaube fast, es könnte einmal ein *buch* daraus werden'.[38] At the beginning of the 1860s, he published translations of individual poems, chiefly in the respected Bern newspaper *Der Bund*, and in 1861 his long essay on Burns and Hebel appeared. There exists a draft later than this date of the only poem of Burns which Corrodi translated, 'Address to the Tooth-Ache', and in 1870 came the publication of the 34 songs of the *Lieder von Robert*

---

37 Quoted in Kupper, p. 65; in the following, I draw on Kupper's research into Corrodi's knowledge of English and his examination of Corrodi's 'Nachlass' held in the Zentralbibliothek Zürich and the Stadtbibliothek Winterthur; see Kupper, pp. 62–69.

38 ibid, p. 65.

Burns, ins Schweizerdeutsche übertragen. From text comparisons with the originals, it appears probable that Corrodi utilised for the *Lieder* Cunningham's 1842 edition of the *Works of Robert Burns*, one of the six editions which he owned in addition to Lockhart's *Life* and several translations of Burns into German. Even if Corrodi did not own all these publications as he prepared his translations for the *Lieder*, they do provide convincing evidence of a serious interest in Burns.

Since the first publication of Corrodi's view of Burns preceded that of the *Lieder*, it is appropriate to consider at this point his essay *Robert Burns und Peter Hebel. Eine literar-historische Parallele.* Corrodi takes as the first point of parallel between the two poets the proximity of their dates of birth, 1759 and 1760, and both anniversaries one hundred years later being celebrated with pomp and style; both men are held in high esteem in their respective countries; although neither travelled they both succeeded in finding 'die Quelle ächter Poesie' (B 4) in their immediate surroundings; neither man knew of the other and since both served the cause of 'edler Menschlichkeit' Corrodi was of the opinion that it would be useful to present a double portrait of the passionate Scot and the placid Southern German. In fact, more of the essay is devoted to Burns and his life and character than to Hebel.

It has to be said that Corrodi's first description of Burns as a man 'der einst auf den Hügeln Süd-Schottlands seinen Pflug lenkte und Lieder dazu sang' (B 3) does not inspire confidence in what is to follow. But gradually a tolerably differentiated picture begins to emerge. Corrodi shows how Burns acquired his 'Gelehrsamkeit' (B 10) and how, after the death of his father, Burns, as a result of the difficulties of making a living and of the theological disputes in which he was involved, 'kam [...] in äußere und innere gefährliche Kämpfe hinein' (B 12). Corrodi goes to some lengths to set the impact of *Poems Chiefly in the Scottish Dialect* of 1786 in the context of the literature of the time.[39] After its publication, 'ein wahrer Triumphzug' (B 17) ensued in the Scottish capital, but he indicates that Burns was not dazzled by the furore, quoting from the letter to Mrs Dunlop of

30 April 1787 (in German translation, as with all the extracts from Burns's letters): 'I know what I may expect from the world, by and by – illiberal abuse, and perhaps contemptuous neglect'. But Corrodi goes on to suggest that it was not exclusively level-headedness on the part of Burns which led to this view but a dark cast of mind: 'Durch seine Briefe schimmert auch in der heitersten Laune eine düstere, bangende Grundstimmung durch' (B 20) and he quotes the letter of 19 December 1797 to Miss Chalmers in which Burns claims to be in a state of 'frequent defeat' in the 'perpetual warfare' between imagination and wisdom. In contrast to the cheerful contentedness of Hebel, Burns 'will [...] immer über seine Sphäre hinausstreben, er weiss oft selber nicht wohin' (B 23). Corrodi mentions 'die mühsam selbsterringende Anstrengung des Autodidakten, wie Burns war' (B 25) and is touched by Burns's orders to his Edinburgh bookseller for books which had to be read in rare periods of free time.

The acceptance by Burns of a post in the excise service is commented on ironically by Corrodi as evidence of his shortcomings as a farmer and his strengths as a poet:

> Ein ächter Bauer [...] wird nie den Pflug stehen lassen und sich unter einen Baum setzen, um ein Maßliebchen zu besingen, das er beim Pflügen umwarf, oder ein Feldmäuslein poetisch zu beklagen, dessen Nest seine Pflugschar zerstörte...Solche Gefühlssubtitilitäten kennt ein wärschhafter Bauer gar nicht. (B 26–27)

The fact that Corrodi highlights this disjunction in Burns renders more complex the simplistic picture of the singing ploughman of the first paragraph of the essay. And Corrodi was almost certainly

39 Modern scholars point to the manner in which the Burns legend excises the poet from his context: 'A poet who had himself a very keen appreciation of his position within a continuing tradition of Scots writing, has been equated with our entire National Literature', R. D. S. Jack and Andrew Noble, 'Introduction' to *The Art of Robert Burns*, ed. by R. D. S. Jack and Andrew Noble (London/Totawa, N.J.: Vision Press/Barnes & Noble, 1982), pp. 7–21 (p. 20).

drawing on his own experience as an artist and writer when he wrote contemptuously of contemporaries of Burns who felt that the poet should confine himself to writing in his spare time: 'Nebenbei könne er ja immer noch dichten! – Nebenbei. Die alte bekannte Geschichte' (B 26). Corrodi also rejects any trivialisation of Burns's work when he emphasises the depth and strength of the Scottish poet: 'Die allermeisten seiner Lieder [sind] nicht im mindesten [...] für Albums und höhere Töchterschulen' (B36). Yet the contrast to Hebel is too pat: if characteristics of the German are 'fröhlicher Lebensgenuß und ruhige Hoffnung auf die Zukunft', those of the Scot are 'wildes leidenschaftliches Ringen mit sich selbst und banger Ausblick in die kommenden Zeiten' (B 23). And when Corrodi writes: 'Burns' ergreifendstes, gewaltigstes Lied, der schottische Kampfhymnos [presumably 'Scots, wha hae'], wurde zu Pferde gedichtet in rasendem Sturmwetter' (B 35–36), it is easy to agree with the view that Corrodi is presenting in Burns a 'Sturm-und-Drang-Auffassung vom dichterischen Genie',[40] for his description inevitably recalls scenes from Schiller's *Die Räuber.* At the same time, it is not true, in my opinion, that Corrodi's picture of Burns in this essay one-sidedly follows Henry Mackenzie's famous designation of Burns, in his 1786 review of the *Poems,* as 'this heaven-taught ploughman'.[41] Certainly, the picture which Corrodi draws for his readers is overblown and owes a great deal to Romantic notions of the creative spirit. But within these parameters, he conveys a good idea of Burns's stature and importance. He closes by extolling the all-embracing 'Humanität' (B 40) of both Hebel and Burns: 'Nichts was Existenz hat ist ihnen gleichgültig' (B 41) and by pointing to the timeless work which they have managed to create from their particular time: 'Burns und Hebel haben den Besten ihrer Zeit genug gethan, und darum haben sie gelebt für alle Zeiten' (B 42). At the same time, Corrodi is definitely of the opinion

40 Kupper, p. 67.
41 Quoted in John D. Ross (ed.), *Early Critical Reviews on Robert Burns* (Glasgow/Edinburgh: William Hodge, 1900), pp.1–7 (p.6).

that Burns is the more important figure: 'Burns bietet [...] viel mehr allgemein Menschliches, er durchläuft die ganze Scala menschlicher Empfindungen und Gefühle weit öfter rein gedanklich als Hebel' (B 39–40). Mackenzie's oft-quoted phrase obscures the fact that he also recognised that Burns was 'a genius of no ordinary rank' whom it behoved his countrymen 'to cherish'.[42] Eighty years later Corrodi might not have provided a radically different view of the stature of the poet from that offered by Mackenzie, but he was communicating his enthusiasm for the greatness of Burns to a German-speaking public against the yardstick of a literary figure familiar to it.

The 'Einführung' to the *Lieder* of 1870 reinforces this enthusiasm by making its recipient a Mr Scrutton, an 'Oxonian' (L 9), whom Corrodi, in an excellent example of how to create a captive audience, has taken out in a rowing-boat on the Lago di Poschiavo at the southern extremity of the Canton of Graubünden.[43] Corrodi recites lines from Burns and asks his guest rhetorically: 'Glauben Sie mir, herr, dass mir von jeher das schottische meiner muttersprache eigenthümlich nahe verwandt erschien?' (L 9). This linguistic kinship between Scots and German-Swiss dialect is developed as a theme in the 'Einführung'. After citing examples of etymological similarities and after claiming that German-Swiss probably derive greater pleasure from Burns than English people, Corrodi continues:

> Nicht das meiste, aber vieles bei ihm [Burns] lässt sich nur in's schweizerdeutsche, präciser nur in's zürichdeutsche[44] unbeschädigt übertragen, wird, in hochdeutscher Küche zubereitet, manchmal geradezu ungeniessbar. Es wölbt sich eine unsichtbare brücke zwischen diesen beiden mundarten und herz und sinn ziehen darauf herüber und hinüber. (L10)

42 Quoted in Ross, pp. 2, 7.

43 This area became much more accessible after the completion of the road over the Bernina Pass in 1865.

44 Kupper, p. 36, states that it is more exact to say that Corrodi has rendered Burns into the 'Winterthurer-Dialekt'.

Corrodi here seems to be arguing that dialect is only fully trans-
latable, not into standard language, but into another dialect, a view
upon which Gottfried Keller, in a letter of 1875, pours scorn in
general terms and also with particular reference to Corrodi: 'In Zürich
haben wir einen solchen Dialektvirtuosen, der hat den Robert Burns
in den Zürcher Landdialekt übersetzt und behauptet, nur in diesem
werde der schottische Dichter wieder genießbar!'[45] Yet Corrodi, still
addressing Mr Scrutton, is also aware of the limitations of dialect:

> Das höchste und das feinste kann sie [dialect] nicht sagen: für das eine
> ist sie zu einfach und für das andere zu schüchtern. Und nehmen Sie
> Burns. Wo er pathetisch wird, da gebraucht er auch richtig meistens
> das reine englisch. (L 10)

Insofar as he acknowledges that the standard language has a wider
range, Corrodi does not seem to be associating himself fully with
proponents of dialect who use it 'als Anbiederungsmittel an sprach-
schützlerische Kreise oder an ein gewisses "Heimat-Publikum"'.[46]
In his monograph on Burns and Hebel, Corrodi had already acknowledged the quality of existing High German translations and did not
seem to be suggesting that a translation into dialect was necessarily
superior to these:

> Wir haben ganz ausgezeichnete Uebertragungen in's Hochdeutsche von
> Freiligrath, Heinze, Bartsch, Kaufmann x.; mir will aber scheinen, als
> passe, wenn doch übersetzt werden muß, gerade unsere alemannische
> Mundart dazu vortrefflich. Beide Idiome haben eine gewisse organische
> Verwandtschaft und es zeigen sich auch zahlreiche überraschende
> Sprachähnlichkeiten. (B 37)

Yet for the reader of 1870 unfamiliar with the first publication of
the monograph nine years previously, the effect of the 'Einführung'
is strongly to underline an emotional affinity between the two small

---

45 Letter to Emil Kuh, 28 June 1875, in Carl Helbling (ed.), *Gottfried Keller.
    Gesammelte Briefe*, 4 vols (Bern: Benteli, 1953), III i, (p. 196).
46 Kupper, p. 34.

countries, the presence of Mr Scrutton not only a reminder of the great English-speaking British Empire but also evoking thoughts of the German-speaking Deutsches Reich created at the end of the year in which the *Lieder* were published.

A second point which might occur to the reader of today is that the 'Einführung' provides absolutely no information on Burns himself. This lack seems unlikely to have arisen from Corrodi's own lack of knowledge since it is reasonable to suppose, from the evidence quoted above, that Corrodi was well-informed. Perhaps Corrodi was assuming some knowledge of Burns in his readers for by 1870 there had been since Kaufmann's book of translations in 1839 no less than seven other books of translations into German devoted exclusively to Burns many of which contained biographical sketches. Additionally, many translations of individual poems had appeared in compendia with biographical notes. Thus Corrodi's assumption was not ill-founded and its basis is possibly indicative of the interest in Burns in German-speaking Europe in the second half of the nineteenth century.

As the title *Lieder* indicates, Corrodi's selection is confined to the songs of Burns, four of the thirty-four chosen not being listed amongst the 'Dubia' in James Kinsley's authoritative *Complete Poems & Songs*.[47] The selection comprises largely love-songs, many of which are well-known: 'A red, red Rose', 'O Whistle, and I'll come to ye, my Lad', 'Jamie come try me', 'John Anderson, my jo' as well as other standards such as 'My Heart's in the Highlands' and 'Auld lang syne'. The 'Einführung' provides no information about the criteria for the selection but approximately eighty-five per cent of Kupper's catalogue of the published and completed unpublished translations made by Corrodi[48] is accounted for by those contained in the *Lieder*. It therefore seems reasonable to claim that the *Lieder* represent a fair reflection of Corrodi's interest in Burns's work. The

47 James Kinsley (ed.), *Burns. Complete Poem & Songs* (Oxford: OUP, 1971).

reader of 1870 is of course made aware neither of this nor of the fact
that Burns wrote anything other than songs. Corrodi's presuppositon
of knowledge and awareness of Burns in his reader is therefore fairly
comprehensive.

Corrodi was not the only Swiss to make translations of Burns
(his countryman Heinrich Leuthold translated some twenty poems
into High German during the 1860s), nor was he the first to publish
translations into dialect (four selections of translations into German
dialects, three in anthologies, one in book form, had already appeared) but he was the first, and to date the only person to translate
Burns into Swiss dialect. Eight years after Corrodi's death, *Lieder* is
referred to by a Scottish critic as being of as high a standard as other
translations into 'Teutonic languages':

> In all the translations we have seen into Teutonic languages – the
> English, German, Dutch, Swedish, Danish and German-Swiss –
> the peculiar metrical forms of Burns are strictly preserved, and it
> would be almost as easy and as pleasant to sing any of the songs in
> German as in the original, making due allowance, of course, for the
> translation.[49]

Arguably, this is an opinion which, while providing evidence of an
awareness of Corrodi's work, is too undifferentiated to be of much
value. Three years later, in the centenary year of Burns's death, however, there is a much more serious assessment. William Jacks, in his
extensive study *Robert Burns in Other Tongues*, devotes a chapter to
Corrodi's *Lieder*. Since it is unlikely that Jacks was fully conversant
with Swiss dialect, it is worth indicating how Jacks assessed the value
of Corrodi's translations or indeed of others, the language of which
he either did not know or knew imperfectly. He writes that he had
these pieces

---

49 Muir, p. 234; on the other hand, Kupper, p. 136, points to the fact that
    most of Corrodi's translations, whatever their other qualities, cannot be
    sung.

retranslated literally into a language which [he] did understand, and the retranslation was sent to a native of the particular country for confirmation and comment, and in this way [he] was able to make [his] remarks.[50]

Judged on the basis of this methodology, Corrodi's *Lieder* emerges very positively.

Jacks selects eight translations, i.e. almost a quarter of the number published, for comment and in each case he prints Corrodi's text in its entirety below his remarks. The first translation, of 'A Man's a Man for a' that', he finds 'almost perfect' and, uniquely in his commentaries, draws a parallel between the country of origin and the country of reception: it is appropriate that what Jacks calls 'this Marseillaise of humanity, the production of Scotland' should be 'so well clothed in the drapery of the language of that country which so much resembles her in efforts brave and bold for Liberty – social, political and religious',[51] a reading of Swiss history which would doubtless have pleased the Romantic ideals of Corrodi. Other translations selected by Jacks fare equally well: that of 'Whistle o'er the Lave o't' is 'very faithfully and well rendered', that of 'John Anderson, my Jo' 'really excellent' and 'To Mary in Heaven' 'in its Swiss mould is a simple and beautiful song'.[52] Jacks points out errors of translation, too, notably in 'Auld lang Syne' and 'Coming thro' the Rye'. Most interestingly, however, Jacks takes Corrodi to task on a point which Corrodi made much of in his 'Einführung' to the *Lieder*, the supposed affinity between Scots and Swiss dialect: in the translation of 'Duncan Gray' Jacks regrets 'that a language which the translator urges to be so similar to broad Scotch could not yield better imagery than the following' and goes on to cite four cases of what for him are feeble renderings, a point wholly consistent with Jacks's observation at the beginning of the chapter on Corrodi which

50 Jacks, p. viii.
51 ibid, pp.158, 159.
52 ibid, pp.164, 166, 167.

challenges Corrodi's assertion of a special affinity: 'While there is a resemblance between many words, this does not seem to exist to any much greater extent than in the other dialects of German'.[53] Jacks does not sum up his findings on Corrodi's translations, but it is clear that, towards the end of the nineteenth century, he provides a not uncritical assessment of Corrodi's undertaking.

Corrodi's contribution to the perception of Burns in German-speaking Europe in the nineteenth century has in my opinion two main features. Firstly, the *Lieder* convey a very clear sense of the strength of Burns, if not of his full range. The translations are for the most part lively and expressive and impart to the German-Swiss reader a good feeling for the originality of the Scottish poet who wrote within a folk tradition. Secondly, Corrodi offers some corrective to the picture of the untutored genius. Inevitably, he saw in Burns, as did the whole of the nineteenth century, what he wanted to see. Robert Walser describes ironically how the poets of the past are usurped to confirm contemporary views: 'Von ihnen [past poets] geht ein wundersames Aladdinlicht aus, das die Treppen, Gänge und Stuben der Zivilisation und der Bildung festlich beleuchtet'.[54] Thus Burns could be held up for much of the nineteenth century to German-speaking readers as a prime example of the fashionable and condescending bourgeois concept of the 'Naturdichter', which Albert Traeger so excoriated. The picture of Burns presented by Corrodi, principally in his monograph, is strongly, but by no means exclusively, influenced by this concept which was so much part of the cultural ethos. But the presentation also drew on Corrodi's own experience and shows a considerable understanding of the problems of the creative writer which Burns was. Overblown in some respects, Corrodi's perception of Burns is above all enthusiastically cognisant of the stature of the Scot.

53 ibid, pp. 162–63, pp. 157–58.
54 Robert Walser, 'Etwas von der Schande', in Robert Walser, *Das Gesamtwerk in 12 Bänden*, ed. by Jochen Greven (Zürich/Frankfurt a.M.: Suhrkamp, 1978), X, pp. 233–36 (p. 235).

It has been claimed that, after the centenary year of 1896, the nineteenth-century perception of Burns rapidly became outmoded as the twentieth century brought new views of the writer, that interest in Burns in German-speaking Europe started to wane at this point and that the works of Burns are today little known there.[55] If this is true, the *Lieder* of the German-Swiss August Corrodi have proved modestly resilient against this general background of decline. The book had new editions in 1940, in 1971 (with a print-run of 800) and in 1998 (with one of 150 copies).[56] Corrodi, in his monograph, had taken issue with narrow readings of Burns which belittled the greatness of the Scot's 'wahre Poesie', for the effect of which on the reader Corrodi cites Goethe's description in *Dichtung und Wahrheit*: 'Wie ein Luftballon hebt sie [die wahre Poesie] uns mit dem Ballast, der uns anhängt, in höhere Regionen, und läßt die verwirrten Irrgänge der Welt in Vogelperspektive vor uns entwickelt daliegen' (B 36). Set in the context of this splendid image, Corrodi's work on behalf of Burns constitutes a very powerful gesture of recognition from one culture to another, from Switzerland to Scotland, and it is altogether appropriate that the *Lieder* are still in print.

55 See Kupper, pp. 9, 48, 171.
56 Kupper, p. 209; information from the Althea Verlag, Zürich, 2005.

Contributors

Joy Charnley (j.charnley@strath.ac.uk) is Lecturer in French at the University of Strathclyde and her research focuses on the work of French-speaking Swiss women writers, in particular Yvette Z'Graggen and Anne-Lise Grobéty. She co-edited five volumes of the *Occasional Papers in Swiss Studies* and is currently finishing a book on Yvette Z'Graggen.

Kate Griffiths (k.griffiths@bangor.ac.uk) is Lecturer in Romance Studies at the University of Wales, Bangor, where she teaches courses in French language, literature and film. She has published on Emile Zola and the cinematic adaptations of his texts and is currently writing a book entitled *Emile Zola: Authorship, Imitation and Adaptation*.

Tom Hubbard (tfhubbard@yahoo.co.uk) is an Honorary Fellow of the Universities of Edinburgh and Glasgow. He was the first Librarian of the Scottish Poetry Library (1984–92), and was editor of the *Bibliography of Scottish Literature in Translation* (2000–04). He has taught at a number of European and American universities and in 2006 he takes up a senior research scholarship at the University of Budapest. He has published his own poetry as well as translations of Swiss and Hungarian poets, including *Poetry from Switzerland* (2002) and *At the End of the Broken Bridge* (2005).

Donal McLaughlin (donal@neilpaterson.net) was in 2003 Scottish PEN's first-ever *écrivain sans frontières* and a winner of the prestigious Robert Louis Stevenson Memorial Award. In 2004, he became the first-ever 'Scottish Writing Fellow' of the City of Bern in Switzerland and was a writer-in-residence at Ledig House (Ghent, New York).

Known for his short stories, he has recently completed his first novel, *Lanzarote*. Donal also translates from German and, in 2003, received an award from the Bundeskanzleramt in Vienna for his work on Stella Rotenberg. He has also edited selections of contemporary writing from Scotland, Slovenia and Latvia.

Thérèse Moreau (therese.moreau@bluewin.ch) was born in Paris and has lived since 1981 in Pully (Switzerland). She took a PhD in Romance languages and Feminist Theory at the John Hopkins University and taught in Kentucky, Maryland and France. Since she has been in Switzerland her main activities have been creative writing and the promotion of a non-sexist French language. She is a fervent reader of English Literature, especially 19th century gothic novels and romantic poetry, Virginia Woolf and modern thrillers. She is the author of *Amanda ou ce fruit maudit de vos entrailles,* a modern gothic novel and of *Le Grand Livre des Recettes Secrètes* which was translated into American English and published by the University Press of the South.

Malcolm Pender (m.j.pender@strath.ac.uk) is Emeritus Professor of German Studies at the University of Strathclyde in Glasgow. His main research interests are in literature in German after 1945, with special reference to the literature of German-speaking Switzerland on which he has published extensively; his last book was *Contemporary Images of Death and Sickness: A Theme in German-Swiss Literature* (1998); he was also co-editor of the series, *Occasional Papers in Swiss Studies,* published under the aegis of the Centre for Swiss Cultural Studies in the Department of Modern Languages at the University of Strathclyde.

Felicity Rash (f.j.rash@qmul.ac.uk) is Reader in German at Queen Mary, University of London. Her main research interests are the sociolinguistics of Switzerland and German-Swiss literature, on which she has published widely; her book *The German Language in Switzerland: Multilingualism, Disglossia and Variation* (1998) has become a standard text and appeared in German translation in 2002; her latest book, *The Language of Violence: Adolf Hitler's 'Mein Kampf'*, is currently in press.

Silvia Ricci Lempen (silvia.ricci@bluewin.ch) was born in Rome in 1951 and has lived in Switzerland since 1975. She has a PhD in Philosophy and for many years was editor of the feminist monthly *Femmes Suisses* (now called *L'Emilie*) then in charge of cultural affairs on the newspapers *Journal de Genève* and *Le Temps*. She is currently teaching a course on gender and culture at the University of Lausanne. She published an autobiographical work in 1991 (*Un homme tragique*, which won the Prix Michel-Dentan), followed by two novels (*Le Sentier des Éléphants*, 1996, awarded the Prix Schiller and *Avant*, 2000, which won the Prix Paul-Budry). She is currently continuing her work as a novelist.

Laura Rorato (mls023@bangor.ac.uk) is Lecturer in Italian at the University of Wales, Bangor, where she teaches courses in Italian language, literature and film. She has published articles on various contemporary writers and co-edited a volume on Postmodern Italian fiction. She is also working on a monograph devoted to literary representations of the life and paintings of Caravaggio.

Sue Wilson (s.wilson14@ntlworld.com) is Senior Lecturer in Design History in the Textile Department at Chelsea College of Art and Design, University of the Arts London. She is currently engaged in doctoral research investigating *The Nineteenth Century English Swiss Cottage* in English domestic architecture and her research interests include International Arts and Crafts and Vernacular Architecture.